Simon Featherstone @HHL
SWAS

8.95

Management of Systems Development

Please Return!

Hutchinson Computer Studies Series

Basic Systems Analysis
Barry S. Lee

Basic Systems Design
Joseph E. Downs

Case Exercises in Computing
Edited by Barry S. Lee

Computer Appreciation and BASIC programming
Allan D. McHattie and Jennifer M. Ward

Microprocessors and Industrial Control
Colin S. Wheeler

Computer Systems: Software and architecture
John L. Newman

Computing in a Small Business
Howard Horner

Data Processing Methods
Barry S. Lee

Fundamentals of Computing
Neil A. Sheldon

Information Systems
Ian A. Beeson

Introduction to Program Design, An
Rod S. Burgess

Scientific Programming
William M. Turner

Structured Program Design Using JSP
Rod S. Burgess

Management of Systems Development

Robert Bell

Principal Lecturer, Department of Mathematics and Computer Studies,
Sunderland Polytechnic

Hutchinson

London   Melbourne   Sydney   Auckland   Johannesburg

Hutchinson Education

An imprint of Century Hutchinson Ltd
62–65 Chandos Place, London WC2N 4NW

Century Hutchinson Australia Pty Ltd
PO Box 496, 16–22 Church Street, Hawthorn,
Victoria 3122, Australia

Century Hutchinson New Zealand Ltd
PO Box 40–086, Glenfield, Auckland 10, New Zealand

Century Hutchinson South Africa (Pty) Ltd
PO Box 337, Bergvlei, 2012 South Africa

First published 1987

Typeset in 10 on 11½pt Plantin by
D.P. Media Limited, Hitchin, Hertfordshire

Printed and bound in Great Britain by
Anchor Brendon, Essex

British Library Cataloguing in Publication Data

Bell, Robert
    Management of systems development.——
    (Hutchinson computer studies series).
    1. Management information systems
    I. Title
    658.4′038   T58.6

ISBN 0-09-165321-5

Contents

Editor's note

This book is one of a series of textbooks with a modular structure aimed at students of computer studies and designed for use on courses at most levels of academic and professional qualification. A coherent approach to the development of courses in computing has emerged over the last few years with the introduction of the BTEC National, Higher National and Post-Experience Awards in Computer Studies. The syllabus guidelines for these courses have provided the focus for this series of books, and this ensures that the books are relevant to a wide range of courses at intermediate level.

Many existing books on computing cause frustration to teachers and students because, in trying to be all embracing, they usually include irrelevant material and fail to tackle relevant material in adequate depth. The books in this series are specific in their treatment of topics and practical in their orientation. They provide a firm foundation in all the key areas of computer studies, which are seen as: computer technology; programming the computer; analysing and designing computer-based systems; and applications of the computer.

Currently there are fourteen books in the series. *Computer Appreciation and BASIC Programming* is the introductory book. It is intended to put the computer into context both for the layman who wants to understand a little more about computers and their usage, and for the student as a background for further study.

Computing in a Small Business is aimed specifically at the small businessman, or at the student who will be working in a small business, and sets out to provide a practical guide to implementing computer-based systems in a small business. It is a comprehensive treatment of most aspects of computing.

Fundamentals of Computing looks in considerably more depth than the previous two books at the basic concepts of the technology. Its major emphasis is on hardware, with an introduction to system software. *Computer Systems: Software and architecture* develops from this base and concentrates on software, especially operating systems, language processors and data base management systems; it concludes with a section on networks. *Microprocessors and Industrial Control* aims to provide a fairly complete description and understanding of a general microprocessor-based system with an emphasis on industrial/control applications. Other aspects of computer technology will be addressed by planned books on graphics, real-time embedded systems and robotics/CIM.

Structured Program Design is about how to design computer programs based on the Michael Jackson method. Examples of program code are given in BASIC, Pascal and COBOL, but this is not a book about a programming language. A sequel to this book which concentrates on PASCAL programming using JSP is "Jackson Structured Programming with PASCAL".

Scientific Programming aims to give a broad and practical view of scientific computing, developing necessary concepts while also revealing some of the problems inherent in solution by computer.

Further books are planned in the software area to cover relational databases, system software and software engineering.

Data Processing Methods provides a fairly detailed treatment of the methods which lie behind computer-based systems in terms of modes of processing, input and output of data, storage of data, and security of systems. Several applications are described. *Information Systems* follows it up by looking at the role of data processing in organizations. This book deals with organizations and their information systems as systems, and with how information systems contribute to and effect the functioning of an organization. Two other books are under development in the area of the application of computers to business; one looks at the business environment for computer-based systems, and the other at the use of decision support and expert systems.

Basic Systems Analysis offers an introduction to the knowledge and skills required by a systems analyst with rather more emphasis on feasibility, investigation, implementation and review than on design. *Basic Systems Design*, the related volume, tackles design in considerable depth and looks at current methods of structured systems design. *Management of Systems Development* aims to give the reader the skills to plan and monitor system development projects as well as an understanding of the policy-making and strategic planning required in information systems development. Further titles in the systems analysis and design area are planned to cover human computer interaction issues and automation of system design.

Case Studies in Business Computing is the final book in the series at the moment, and provides a large number of case studies with questions to provide practical work in most areas of computing work. The exercises are all based on real life, and suggested solutions are available separately to bona fide teachers.

The books in this series stand alone, but all are related to each other so that duplication is avoided.

Barry S. Lee
Series editor

List of tables

List of figures

Preface

This book is primarily designed for students following BTEC courses in Computer Studies. In addition it is hoped that the structure of the text is such that it will act as a framework for undergraduate studies in the area. In both cases the material contained here will easily be assimilated by students who have completed a period of industrial training and are therefore familiar with a systems development environment. Part-time students and other junior practitioners are also suitably placed to obtain benefit by the study of selected chapters.

Two arguments for including management topics in a higher education course in computing are advanced. First, students are made aware of the objectives which their future managers will be trying to achieve. This preparation will educate students to the purpose of the management actions which they will observe, and will help to secure their understanding and support for these actions. Secondly, it is necessary to recognize the rapid career movements which occur for people employed in systems development, particularly in small organizations. The corporate awareness and planning skills acquired by a study of the management task are, in the case of some students, likely to be required soon after leaving their higher education course.

The structure of the book is a top down treatment of management, starting with matters of strategic concern, continuing to the organization of systems development departments and on to the tactics of project management. Within this framework systems development processes appear roughly in the order in which they occur in the life cycle. However, some topics do not easily fit this idealized arrangement. For instance, the activity needed to procure a major computer configuration or enhancement often relates not to a single application area but to a forecast of the workload across a range of dissimilar applications. This activity therefore does not relate to the idea of a single system life cycle. Procurement is, however, related to the actions needed in feasibility studies, and I have therefore discussed it within Chapter 2. Some topics occur under more than one heading, e.g. maintenance is discussed from two perspectives:

staff organization in Chapter 3 and control aspects in Chapter 7.

Chapter 1 connects organizations with the information systems that they use. The objective is to show how an organization ensures that those application systems identified for development are relevant, timely and responsive to widely viewed needs.

Chapter 2 shows how major investments in application systems are assessed and identifies the key role for users at the very beginning of development.

Chapter 3 identifies structures and standards for the systems development workforce and discusses their relationships with user groups.

Chapters 4 and 5 are concerned with the techniques used to manage projects including a review of likely problems and possible actions.

Chapter 6 looks at staff motivation, leadership and career development for staff working in information systems.

Chapter 7 concentrates on the post-construction phase of systems development where systems are made live and then continually adjusted in response to the changing user world in which they operate.

In general, the book assumes that the reader views systems development from the standpoint of one working in a medium-to-large information systems department which is itself part of a greater organization. For other readers (e.g. those in a very small systems group or a software house) some topics may be irrelevant (e.g. charge out and budgetary mechanisms) or over elaborate (e.g. the recruitment process). I feel, however, that much that is contained here can be applied wherever management of information systems development takes place.

Each chapter finishes with some questions which it is hoped will help the reader to explore and apply the information contained in that chapter.

1 Policies and plans

Introduction

It is not always obvious to the person writing the COBOL statement, but it is almost certain that the act of coding can be linked back to an overall plan formulated to ensure the survival and success of the organization as a whole. The purpose of this chapter is to begin to explore that linkage by looking at strategic planning in organizations with reference to the role for computer-based information systems.

If the existence of planning is not obvious, then the justification for it may be similarly obscure. Perhaps the biggest credibility gap of all exists for *strategic* planning. How can one seriously talk about five year plans in a business which changes as fast as computing? The answers to these doubts are discussed in detail later in this chapter, but confidence in the relevance of strategic planning can be gained by looking at the consequences of not having overall objectives. How would we deal with the clamour of user departments' needs? How would we evaluate and control the flood of computing products and salespersons? How would we put in place systems which can evolve with an organization as it responds to its growth plan? How would we ensure that systems allow people's jobs to remain worthwhile? In fact for many large organizations, five years could be the span of a single project, and the sort of strategic planning we are to discuss may be performed for time spans of eight or ten years.

Another reason for doubt about strategic planning is based on the general dislike of planning by those on the receiving end. Where strategic planning is concerned the recipients are the whole of the systems development workforce. How unpleasant to have one's choice of hardware and software products constrained by company purchasing policy. How time-wasting to have to respond to standards in the production of user requirement specifications. How irritating to have to customize a purchase ledger package when so many other interesting systems are waiting to see the light of day. There is no easy way to enliven the implementation of strategic plans. Compared with the thrill of seeing one's modules of code bringing benefit to the workplace, strategic plans are relatively unexciting. Employees in an organization which has a sensible and widely communicated information systems strategy will unconsciously understand and accept the relevance of what they are doing. They will see most short term planning announcements as conforming to their understanding of where the organization is heading. Employees in less fortunate circumstances may find the relevance of their day-to-day work, and the actions of their management, incomprehensible.

Hierarchy of plans

Constructing an information systems strategy is only one of several planning activities that take place within an organization. Its position in the hierarchy of planning is shown in Figure 1.1. The input comes from the overall strategy for the organization, a variety of external factors and the current status of the systems within the organization. Output from strategic planning consists of an applications master plan, a policy statement (covering technology, jobs and people) and schedules for the use of resources (computers, communication equipment, staff, finance). These outputs in their turn give rise to individual feasibility studies according to a specific implementation priority. After a positive feasibility study further planning will then give rise to networks, bar charts, computer usage plans, cost plans and task sheets for individual development staff.

This then, in planning terms, is the linkage between the person writing the COBOL statement and the upper reaches of the organization's management. It is an idealized picture and few organizations will conform to it in every particular. Sometimes strategies are not at

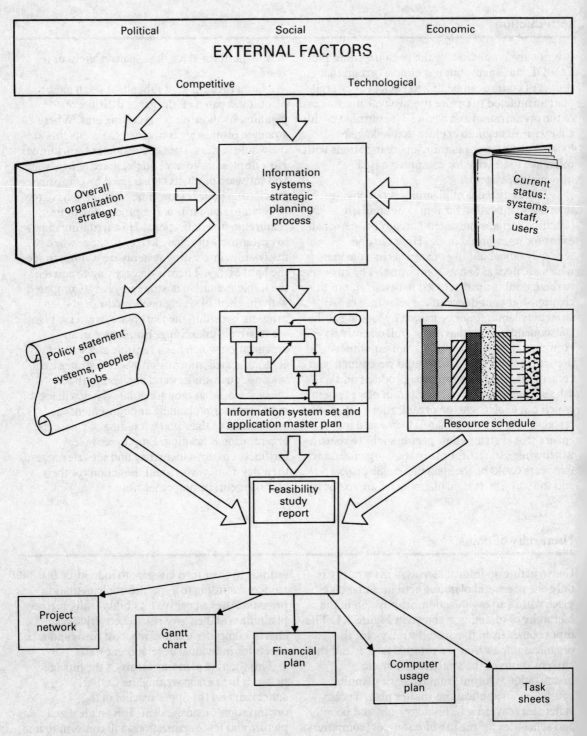

Figure 1.1   *Hierarchy of plans*

all clearly stated, for several reasons. Perhaps the organization has such an obvious single objective that nothing needs to be stated. Or senior management may deliberately withold their overall strategy from publication, to maintain the best position against competitors or to minimize the potential loss of bargaining power with suppliers, or trades unions. Whatever the reason, without an explicit overall strategy a team engaged in the construction of an information system strategy is in real difficulty. It may be reduced to putting together a series of alternatives based on hunches, from which senior management will select the one preferred. While this may produce a plan, it will not be clear how the plan has evolved and those working on development projects may be denied that overall sense of direction which is so beneficial to their motivation.

Influences on the information systems strategy

Overall organization strategy
One major influence on an information systems strategy will always be the organization's overall strategy, and an important component of this is the style in which the organization offers its goods or services to the customer. In the case of private organizations there are many styles and each has a set of implications for the types of information

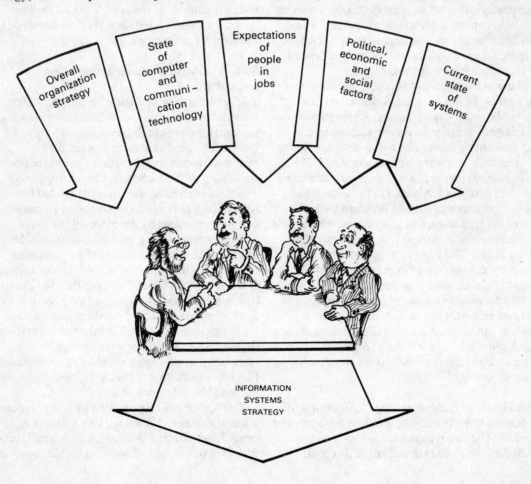

system needed and the way in which they should be developed. Two examples are given below.

Service style A: Production efficiency This type of organization concentrates on offering low prices and a fast service in a specific market, probably with a limited range of popular standard products. The strategic role for their systems must therefore be to provide efficient monitoring of production and to maintain accurately, stock at a carefully calculated level. Systems will probably have to be tailored precisely to the organization, which will be prepared to invest heavily to get them right.

Service style B: Customer requirements This type of organization is prepared to design, tailor and manufacture according to each customer's needs. The strategic role for systems in this environment will be to control contract costs carefully. These will be archived, and the organization's ability to prepare accurate contract estimates will depend on their use of this historical data.

Many public organizations (e.g. local authorities, health authorities) serve two masters; the public and the government. A systems strategy must recognize this by addressing the requirements of both. The public requires features such as responsiveness and accountability, resulting in the systems becoming rich with complex facilities. On the other hand the government will continually introduce changes of legislation and procedures, which must be incorporated into these same systems, often very quickly. The strategy must therefore ensure that pools of expertise exist in key application areas to balance these twin pressures.

An organization's strategy contains more than directives on attitudes to customers. It is also likely to contain an indication of the means by which growth is to be achieved. Again, this facet of the strategy has implications for an information systems strategy.

Growth style A: Expanding range. Growth is to be achieved by diversifying into new products and services. The role for information systems is to assist decision makers in pursuit of this goal.

Computer-based models may be found useful in assessing markets and in predicting the performance of products or services.

Growth style B: Acquire new divisions. Growth is to be achieved by buying and absorbing small companies with good potential. The organization will become a carefully controlled federation of separately operating units. Information systems will be important at two levels. First it will be useful to have a set of simple hardware-compatible packages which can be implemented quickly for each new company acquired. Secondly, a flexible financial reporting system capable of collecting and consolidating details across the federation will be essential.

Each facet of an organization's strategy has implications for the information system strategy and may contribute towards decisions on which systems are considered, how they are developed and over what timescale.

State of computer and communications technologies

The reader will be familiar with the gee-whizz statistics of computing. Cost graphs seem to plummet, power graphs seem to soar. The breakneck speed of development in the microelectronics industry forces hardware prices down by 15–20% each year. Computing power which, in the 1960s, was carefully tended by teams of operators in air-conditioned rooms is now outperformed by the power of the microcomputer sitting on the accountant's desk. Cheaper hardware also makes more ambitious software feasible. Technology appears in a series of waves — each benefiting from the ever-cheaper component costs of computing (see Figure 1.2). Each wave has presented or will present a challenge to those managing information systems development. Should new technology be introduced at all? When should it be introduced? Can it coexist with other technologies? Must it be universal in our organization?

The opportunities presented by computer and communications technologies are relevant to many functions within an organization and the inclusion of certain technologies within the terms

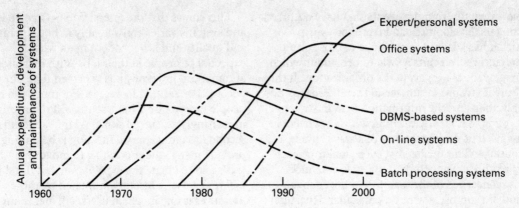

Figure 1.2 *Technology growth patterns*

of reference of the information system strategy may be a matter for discussion. Examples are Computer-Aided Design (CAD), Computer Numerically Controlled (CNC) plant, office systems and computer-controlled communication systems such as a PABX (private automatic branch exchange), and intelligent knowledge-based systems (IKBS).

Individual managers and professionals within the organization often want the independence to choose their own information tools and for this reason may be reluctant to agree to a wide set of terms of reference for the information system strategy. However, the best strategy will always be the widest one and it would be unwise to limit the scope of planning at this, the highest level. Of course, many strategies will recommend that certain divisions within an organization *are* given autonomy over their use of information technology, because this policy is considered the best means of harnessing the skills and energies of the people concerned to achieve the desired information system objectives.

Another factor to be addressed early is the *importance* of information systems to an organization. In certain fields (e.g. banking, insurance, building societies) information systems are of fundamental importance. Often information is the service which identifies the organization and makes it special in the customer's eyes. For organizations of this type, managing each wave of technology is crucial to their position. Each new development must be

monitored, tested and implemented when proven. This argues for special teams of people with the systems development function whose task it is to undertake research, selection and evaluation of each new type of product relevant to their business. Pilot projects are often set up before proliferation of the new technology throughout the organization is attempted. Pioneering organizations of this type have achieved the spread of banking and other specialist terminals linked to large computer/communication networks, and will be behind the introduction of electronic funds transfer systems in the near future.

Organizations for which information systems are less important are usually more cautious about the introduction of a major new technology. They may obtain some benefit from those which are pioneering their way through the early difficulties. The key judgement is whether a particular technology is sufficiently stable and beneficial for incorporation into an information system strategy.

Expectations of people in jobs
Human factors have two slightly different influences on the formation of an information system strategy. The next section is concerned with those factors which are considered external to the organization. This section is concerned with factors which arise from the expectations of people in their jobs within an organization.

Any organization will have a culture which will

have grown up from the events that have occurred during its development and from the way in which it has adapted in response to those events. This culture transmits a style of behaviour which may pervade all or part of the organization. If the culture is strong and universal then there may be implications for the information system strategy. An example is an organization which has become convinced of the importance of always having a pilot stage. This means that every major project will require a planned pilot phase to convince those concerned of the viability of the change. Another example is where a particular department has attained a dominant role in the organization and expects always to lead the field. In the introduction of a new wave of technology (e.g. office automation, expert systems) this department would expect to be the front runner.

The interaction of individuals with systems also needs to be considered. In this context difficulties arise from the changing nature of this interaction. Consider the grid in Figure 1.3.

This shows that the interaction between people and systems varies considerably in both quantity and quality and is dependent upon what is expected of people in their job. With increased automation, however, it is expected that jobs will become less routine in nature. For more and more people interaction with systems will require increasingly advanced skills. At the same time secondary and tertiary education is beginning to provide many students with a foundation in these skills and to create the expectation that the skills will find a use. The climate created by these pressures is one in which users will increasingly expect to be able to exercise discretion in connection with their use of information systems. The implications for the information system strategy are that users should be involved in the selection of hardware and software components, and that software products should allow an ever-expanding group of people to use information systems in complex ways.

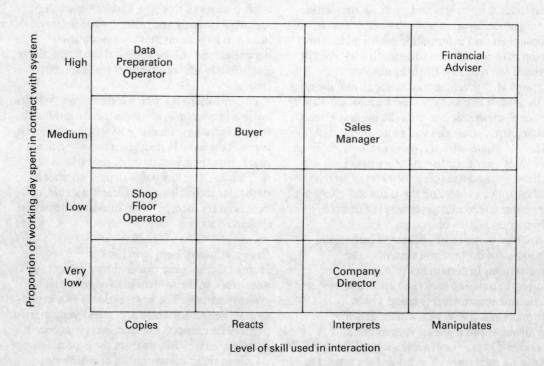

Figure 1.3   *People's interaction with systems*

Political, economic and social factors

Factors outside an organization have an influence on its information system strategy in two ways. First, they will influence the organization's overall strategy (modifying company growth plans, opening new or closing off old markets, encouraging or discouraging employment) and secondly they will have a direct effect on the information system strategy itself.

The factors vary widely both in the size of the impact they have and in the speed of absorption which they require. It is not possible to generalize about these so some examples are given below.

Industrial action in computer operations

In several public sector organizations in recent years there have been disputes between management and computer operations staff resulting in full or partial withdrawal of labour. The effect on the organization has been severe, adversely affecting its cash flow and disrupting the service normally offered. A potential management response to this state of affairs is to attempt to dissolve the concentration of power in computer departments by establishing an information system strategy which encourages the growth of decentralized systems. Input, processing, output and control for individual systems are entrusted to staff in the user departments concerned.

Competitive tendering for public service work

The pressure on public bodies to open up their service provision to outside contracts has implications for an information system strategy. New systems must be developed and many existing systems modified to reflect a much more detailed concern with quotations for service and the monitoring of costs of that service.

The Data Protection Act

Inevitably the existence of the Data Protection Act has implications for the information systems strategy of many organizations. Some strategic issues that have been considered by organizations closely concerned with the Act are:

The creation of a Data Processing Officer post to oversee interpretation and compliance with the Act.

Recognition that the Act applies to automatic, and not manual data processing systems. Should a new system be put into the Act's sphere of influence (i.e. computerized) or left out?

Of course the Act has implications for other than strategic issues. The impact in areas such as systems design, security and audit will be increasingly felt as further experience is gained.

Current state of systems

We have so far considered a wide range of factors that will influence the formation of an information system strategy, each having a positive emphasis. Each factor, whether it is to do with the availability of some exciting new technology, or the corporate ambition for growth, will provide an argument for change and will promote the evolution of information system usage within the organization. However, the organization is likely to be heavily committed to its current hardware and systems software, its application systems and the people and practices which support them. Any information system strategy worth considering will recognize these commitments and must show how development will take place.

It is rarely possible for an organization to achieve major changes overnight. The plan for change will particularly need to allow time for the personnel involved to absorb necessary information and become effective in the new circumstances. A major difficulty arises when the development involves staffing changes leading to redundancy or unpopular redeployment. Organizations will normally seek to retain, retrain and utilize good staff when possible. If, however, the change does involve staff reduction then the organization will be lucky to control that reduction on its own terms. The use of expensive contract staff may become necessary.

A change in a major hardware or software supplier is never undertaken lightly, and usually takes longer than initially envisaged. There are many good reasons for staying with a particular set of suppliers, including staff experience, the relationship with the supplier's support staff, and the desire to avoid expensive evaluation of alternative suppliers. Doubts about a supplier's long-term commercial viability, however, or the adequacy of its product range will occasionally necessitate a change. In this case the information system strategy must consider the options for system conversion. Can we convert when the current systems require rewriting? Must we move quickly on to the new equipment and, therefore, set up a system conversion 'factory'?

The current application systems themselves will come under close scrutiny and the people responsible for constructing the information system strategy will need access to a recent review of their effectiveness. Many systems will be reviewed because of influences discussed earlier, e.g. they are identified for change because of the

organization's growth plan, or because newly available software can be beneficially exploited. Even if a system does not fall into this category it should not be excluded from a re-examination. It should, in fact, be perfectly possible to terminate an application system which has consistently failed to realize expected benefits and for which there is agreement that no cost-effective redevelopment can be achieved.

We have considered the influence which the status quo has on the information system strategy. It is perhaps no surprise that many of the issues which occur under this heading are to do with people: their legitimate worries, perhaps their inertia and, occasionally, their downright obstructiveness. Great skill will be needed in weaving into the strategy details of the negotiations, the training and information dissemination procedures needed to cope effectively with these issues.

Formation and maintenance of the information systems strategy

The strategy team
The formation of an information system strategy is a key task for any organization. The strategy must be viable and acceptable. Its construction requires attention to the diverse influences discussed in the previous section and the

members of the team charged with that construction must have the skills necessary for the task.

Table 1.1 shows the categories of people from which selection of a strategy team could take place.

Table 1.1   Selection of a strategy team

	Information Systems Group	Systems User Group	Union Representation	External Consultancy
Senior level	Information system management	User department management	Full-time local official	Senior consultant
Middle level	Project leaders, team leaders	Section leaders, foremen	Works convenors, representatives	Specialist consultant
Junior level	Analysts, programmers, operators	Shop floor workers, clerks	Shop stewards, office representatives	—

People from the information systems group will contribute knowledge of current and future technology and a thorough understanding of current application systems. The systems user group understand the organization's methods of business, its plans for the future and the effectiveness of current applications. Union representatives will express the interest of groups and individuals involved. External consultants can bring a fresh and objective view, specific technical skills and experience.

The breadth of outlook and experience required for the strategy planning will be found mainly in the senior and middle levels of each group. However, at the junior level there is a lot of detailed knowledge of current systems which should not be disregarded. It must also be recognized that the eventual strategy will depend on the junior level for its implementation at least as much as any other level. For these reasons, as well as to encourage individuals to exercise some control over their destiny, the view of the junior level managers should be included.

Certain constraints will apply when choosing a team for strategy planning. Although in principle it should express the broadest set of interests, the size of the team should be carefully controlled. Large teams can generate additional administrative work and provide opportunities for personality clashes. Organizations may well have legitimate reasons for narrowing the team down to a small subsection of those represented in Table 1.1. Protection of a competitive position, a history of difficult industrial relations or a statutory requirement to include or exclude certain interests may influence formation of the team. Sometimes the whole task is given to the information system development manager, who must then do his best in the certain knowledge that his output will lack the authority of a more widely based effort.

Format of the information system strategy

There are three main types of output to be expected from the team responsible for producing the information system strategy:

1 Policies which provide guidance for later, more detailed decisions.

2 A specific plan (the *application master plan*) for major system development over the appropriate timespan (normally five years).
3 Schedules for major hardware and software acquisition and manpower usage.

The policies will be formulated into a statement and must communicate the main outputs of the strategic planning process throughout the organization.

First a line of reasoning is drawn which connects the overall organization strategy to the types of system needed to help implement that strategy. Secondly, the selection of a technology base is justified and will include any major migration which has to take place. Decisions on a supplier policy (if any) could also be stated although this will be excluded if it is felt that the organization's negotiating stance will be prejudiced by its inclusion. Thirdly, the statement should specify any overriding principles which will operate during the proposed transformation. For example, if there are no planned changes to the structure or size of the information systems development group or to the wider organization workforce then the statement should clearly say so and remove uncertainty and distrust at the outset. Similarly any conditional elements of the policy should be clear e.g. the decentralization of data processing to individual departments to be instituted when all departments have undertaken sufficient recruitment and training to make them self-supporting. An example of a statement of this type is shown below.

Tenby Holdings plc

Policy for information systems

Issued October 1986
Review October 1987   *Valid* October 1991

Background issues
Key aspects of Tenby's business plan influencing this policy statement are:

1 The trend to a decentralized profit centre

structure for the group is to be accelerated by giving more autonomy to individual divisions, coupled with simple but rigorous group financial management.

2 Growth will be achieved largely by the acquisition of new units, with a bias towards high technology products.

3 A more responsive customer service is needed at Neptronics and Flowmeter. They will hold inventory at higher levels of assembly than previously, and despatch procedures are to be tightened up.

4 Defence contractor quality regulations are to be introduced at Aircontrol.

Distribution of facilities

Decentralization within the group requires that information systems are managed by the operating divisions. The surest way of achieving this is to allocate sufficient resources to enable each division to operate independently in the development and operation of its own systems. Generally, this is to be achieved by fostering the growth of microcomputer networks at each division. The exception is that some of the processing needs of Aircontrol and Flowmeter currently exceed the capabilities of microcomputers. For this reason a mainframe facility is to be retained (and enhanced) to provide for the specialized needs of these two divisions. The cost of the mainframe service will be recovered by internal charges to the two divisions concerned. The mainframe will focus financial reporting, and the costs of this aspect of its work will be borne by Head Office.

Systems development priorities

1 Decentralization is a key issue for the group. The top system development priority must be to support this by the evaluation, selection and implementation of appropriate microcomputer networks. These networks will support all applications for a division (other than previously identified specialized needs). Software tools which permit selected users to develop their own applications will be installed although it is envisaged that some complex applications will require the specialized

development expertise of the Information Systems Development Group. Installation of a pilot network at Neptronics is targetted for November.

2 To support the group growth policy of unit acquisition, a standardized financial reporting system is to be specified. This will detail inward reporting timetables, cut-offs and accuracy parameters. The specification will be such that a manual implementation for emergency use by a newly acquired unit is possible. However, the specification will also be implemented on the selected microcomputer network and it is required that each division adopts this implementation as their networks are installed. Pilot use of the financial reporting system will occur on the pilot network. Full implementation across the group to be achieved by December next. This new approach to group control is intended to provide financial performance figures within ten working days of period end.

3 The inventory control application systems are basically adequate to respond to the new concern for customer services but certain enhancements are required. Customer order progress will be constantly monitored against target dates and hard copy late lists are to be output. Sophisticated printing devices capable of quickly producing these management reports and customer despatch documentation will be installed. Appropriate software enhancements to back this additional hardware will be developed and the whole implementation achieved by December next. The achievement of delivery dates is expected to improve from 65% to 85% of all orders as a result of these enhancements.

4 The applications in use at Aircontrol require rewriting to permit the material traceability required by defence contract regulations. The target is for these applications to pass the external conformity examination by January next.

Information Systems Development Group priorities

Productivity of the ISDG must be examined. Improvements are looked for with respect to both construction and maintenance activity if the group's response to competitive situations and new marketing opportunities is to be properly supported by information systems. This will involve the adoption of a new development framework permitting more rapid responses to user requests. New tools will also be evaluated and the recent successful experiments with close user cooperation in design work will be formalized. The overall objective is to ensure that most user objectives are suitably defined and achieved not more than six months from project inception.

Implications for staff
Most office staff in each division will require training in the use of microcomputers. Some will also receive instruction on how to develop their own applications. Staff in ISDG will provide much of this training and will offer a continuing advice and support service. An internal reorganization of ISDG involving the establishment of specialized user support sections will take place.

It is not anticipated that any net change in staff size will occur as a result of the implementation of this policy. However, job descriptions are to be revised and staff will be fully consulted with respect to any changes in their duties.

The second part of the information system strategy plan concerns the identification of specific major applications to be developed over the period covered by the strategy. This key output is called the application master plan and is discussed in the next section.

The third part of the information system strategy plan concerns schedules showing how resources will be controlled over the period. These may be firm for the next twelve months but less certain further in the future. Examples are:
- A plan for the acquisition of hardware
- A plan for the acquisition of systems software
- A plan for the acquisition of applications packages and development tools
- A manpower usage plan for development and maintenance work
- A financial plan reflecting expenditure of all of the above items.

An example of this type of output is shown in Figure 1.4 (see page 24).

Maintenance of the information system strategy
A five year plan does not last five years! No matter how clear cut an organization's objectives or how stable its circumstances there will be some unforeseen events which will ensure the plan has to be modified. Such events include internal changes such as new key personnel, a new organization structure and sudden changes in profitability; and external changes such as the rapid maturing of a new technology, new government legislation and changes in the economic climate. It is probably wise to review the strategy annually, but circumstances may force a major revision at any time, for example following a merger or takeover.

Maintaining an information system strategy requires the same processes as creating one. Usually, many factors will be unchanged and the process will be simpler. A bulletin describing the progress of the strategy and a restatement of its objectives is useful in keeping those involved up to date.

Application Master Plan

The information systems set
The information systems established within an organization (whether computer-based or not) are coupled together, some more closely than others, into a set which serves the overall information needs of that organization. A general model of

such coupled systems is shown in Figure 1.5.

Decision systems exist to assist senior management in making strategic decisions. Often such systems take the form of a model either of the whole organization or some portion of it and must particularly permit 'what if' type questions

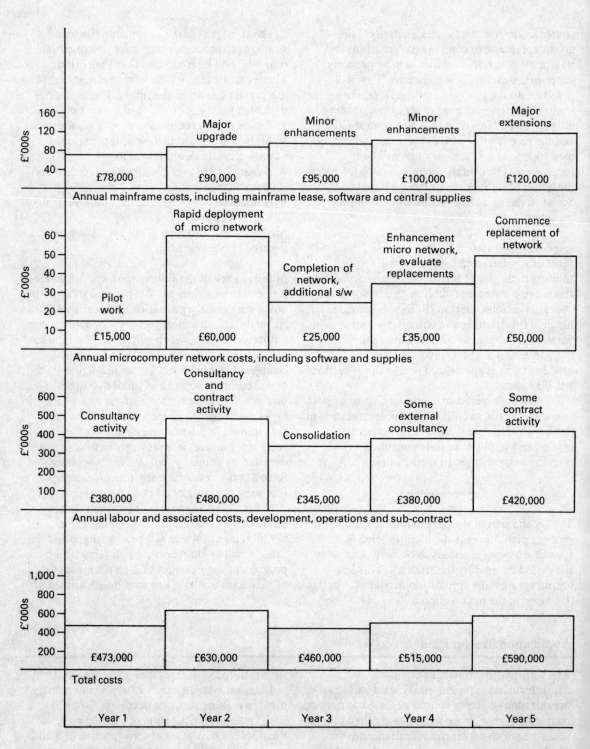

Figure 1.4   *Expenditure plan*

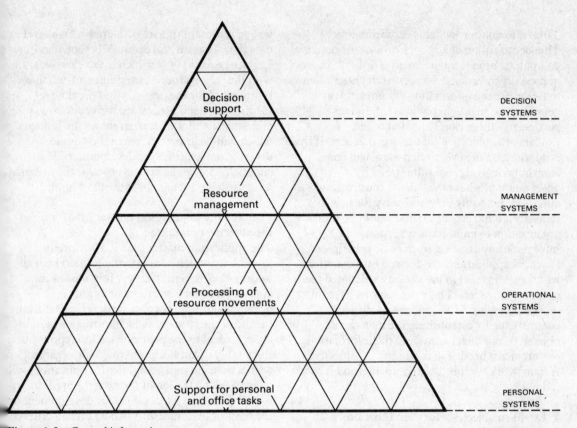

Figure 1.5   *General information systems set*

to be asked. Major product line changes, new interest rate schemes, new acquisitions are examples of types of initiative which must be explored by modelling before a final decision is made.

Management systems are responsible for the control of the organization as it is currently constituted. Used mainly by middle management, these systems must ensure that resources are being used and results achieved in line with plans. In doing this there will be a reliance on report by exception. These systems are characterized by the frequent need to survey or select from a whole data base using criteria preset by management.

Operational systems are responsible for the flow of important messages within the organization (e.g. invoices, clock cards, stock receipts, paying-in slips), and for recording all of these messages and their effects. These systems are also responsible for maintaining the life histories of

entities important to the organization (e.g. employees, customers, suppliers, ratepayers). These systems were among the first established in many organizations and may have had their technology base updated several times.

Personal systems are those which support the information processing required by individuals either for their own personal and professional needs (word processing, appointments diary, calculations, computer-aided design) or for group needs (mail systems, copying and distribution, filing and retrieval of documents, drawings). This category of system is certain to undergo rapid changes as information technology is successfully applied not only to the standard office tasks but also, through use of expert systems, to assist various professionals within the organization (e.g. maintenance engineers, legal executives) to complete their tasks.

Total information systems requirements

The identification of key applications for potential computerization is not normally a difficult process in most organizations. The research undertaken to formulate the information system strategy is very likely to highlight obvious candidates, particularly those closely related to the fundamental objectives of the organization. If this is not the case then very often ideas will come from outsiders (e.g. consultants) or by observation of what others do. A more formal approach, probably only necessary for new or radically altered organizations, would be for the organization to build its own version of an information systems set from basic principles. Potential applications are derived by discussions with key personnel in the various functional areas of the organization. These discussions have much in common with classic systems analysis, commencing by establishing the managerial objectives and then identifying the informational requirements needed to achieve these objectives. A framework for this 'bottom up' method is as follows.

1 Establish objectives for each function.
2 Establish what links exist between a function and other functions – in other words, what inputs and outputs are required in order that objectives can be met?
3 Establish the role which information plays in achieving these objectives, and in maintaining the links.
4 Categorize the information identified above according to the system level which it serves; decision, management, operational, personal.
5 Form a matrix of information requirement and cluster elements in the matrix to define discrete systems.

An example of such a matrix formulated for a company which manufactures for stock against a sales forecast is shown in Table 1.2. Elements of the matrix are examined in turn and potential systems identified by clustering together those elements which have a large number of strong mutual linkages. In this way an organization can create its own information system set. A useful way to represent this set is to draw a high level data flow diagram. An example is shown in Figure 1.6 (see page 28) of just such a data flow diagram with the major processes and information flows represented for the organization previously mentioned. Each process may give rise to a system or systems, and the diagram shows the linkages which will be important when it comes to deciding on priorities for development. For simplicity's sake the systems used at the personal level in Table 1.2 are not shown in Figure 1.6.

Forming the application master plan – role of the steering committee

The application master plan is a key product of the activity which goes into the formation of an information system strategy. It is a list of the applications, each with a priority and a development time span, to be developed during the life of the strategy. The information system set described in the previous section represents the totality of applications which the organization wishes to bring into being. Some applications will already exist – the job of forming the application master plan is to select others for development on the basis of their measure against certain criteria.

This selection devises and presents a schedule for the next stage of the system development process which will almost certainly be a detailed feasibility study for each application in turn.

The criteria to be applied in selecting from the information system set are as follows:

1 *Intrinsic worth* Using the methods and measures approved by the organization for conducting feasibility studies (see Chapter 2) what benefit does a particular application bring?
2 *Strategic worth* Without necessarily having significant quantifiable benefits some applications may be capable of achievements close to the fundamental objectives of an organization.
3 *Foundation value* Some applications are valuable because of the way they enable *others* to be realized.
4 *Potential for balance* In choosing applications for implementation it will often be necessary, for optimum utilization of development staff,

Table 1.2 Matrix of information requiremements

	Financial Function	Sales and Marketing	Research Development Design	Material Control	Manufacturing Control	Supplier Function	Personnel Services
Decision level	1.1 Product/ profitability assessment	1.2 Pricing policies	1.3 Putting products into production	1.4 Choosing inventory levels	1.5 Plant investment	1.6	1.7 Manpower needs
Management level	2.1 Profit and loss Budget monitoring Cost monitoring	2.2 Sales analysis Sales forecasts	2.3 Control of R+D projects	2.4 Stock valuation Requirements planning	2.5 Manufacturing through-put Plant utilization Sub-contracting Quality analysis	2.6 Supplier performance	2.7 Manpower analysis
Operational level	3.1 Sales accounting Supplier accounting Payroll Asset registration Cost collection	3.2 Sales orders Sales order enquiries	3.3 Product manufacture details Product performance	3.4 Stock movements Stock enquiries Stock replenishment orders	3.5 Manufacturing order movements Manufacturing order enquiries Plant status Employee performance Scrap monitoring	3.6 Purchase order creation Purchase order maintenance and monitoring	3.7 Personnel records maintenance and enquiry
Personal level	4.1 Tabulations	4.2 Word processing Export documentation	4.3 Draughting Design calculations	4.4	4.5	4.6 Word processing Supplier contacts database	4.7 Word processing Company standing orders

user staff, computer resources and the observation of political pressures, to create a balanced priority list.

These are complex criteria to apply. It would be wrong (but unfortunately possible) for the information systems development manager to be alone responsible for deducing the various features of each application and applying the selection criteria. The most common means of achieving this is through a steering committee for whom this task of forming the application master plan would be a priority item.

In many organizations the steering committee is the authority under which all information system work takes place. In this case the committee would meet regularly (perhaps quarterly) and when appropriate would set up the working party

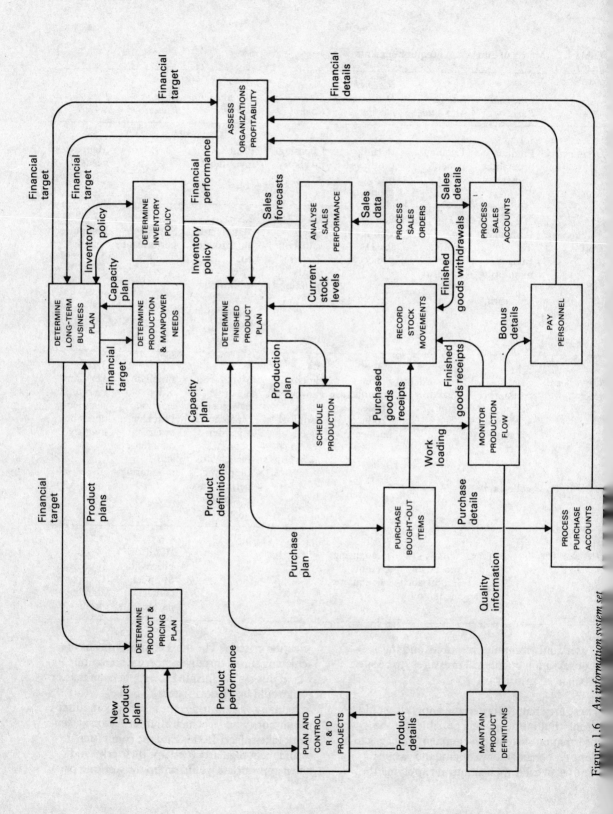

Figure 1.6   *An information system set*

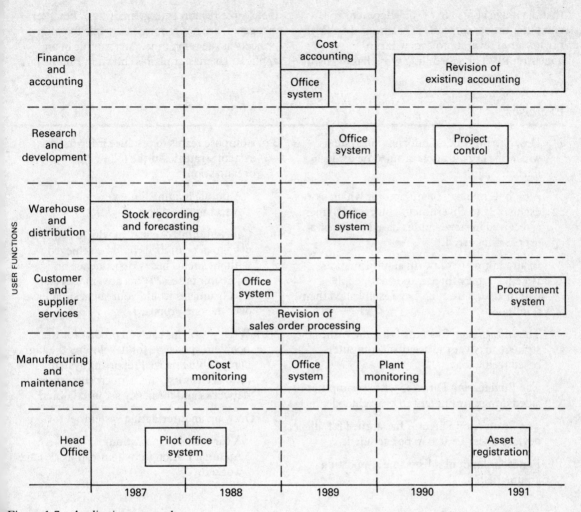

Figure 1.7 *Applications master plan*

needed to review the information system strategy. It would also make minor amendments to components of the strategy between major reviews.

A computer steering committee must be chaired by a senior executive whose objectives are identified with the organization as a whole. Membership should reflect the various interests of the organization and occasional reviews should be undertaken to ensure that major users or intended users have adequate representation. Senior members of the computer staff should also be members.

The task of forming the application master plan will be undertaken by the steering committee by applying the four criteria outlined above. Input from the computer staff representatives will ensure that any feasibility assessment is realistic and that the foundational value of candidate systems is not missed. Users will of course argue the case for applications in their own area and the committee as a whole, guided by the chair will ultimately agree priorities. The computer staff representatives will then schedule each agreed project for its feasibility study stage and will sketch in the remainder of the stages in such a way that the usage of resources (development staff, computer time, user staff) is balanced. In a large organization several projects will run concurrently. The scheduling work has to ensure that scarce resources (e.g. analysts or key user managers) are not required to juggle too many projects at the same time. An example of an applications master plan is shown in Figure 1.7.

Exercises

1   Describe the kind of information systems which the organization profiled below is likely to require.

A high technology manufacturer which works exclusively to government contract. Payment is received in stages and is based on proof of expenses incurred.

2   In attempting to draw up an information system strategy three important people within an organization have established their standpoints:

The Information Systems Director wishes the strategy to cover the use of all computer-based technology.

The Engineering Director wishes computer-aided design equipment to be excluded.

The Production Director has argued for all devices under £5,000 to be excluded.

For each standpoint list some supporting arguments.

3   Compose teams to produce information system strategies at the following organizations:

A public lending library
A technical college

4(a)   Can you think of a way in which Tenby's urge to decentralize could be achieved without such a heavy dependence on microcomputers? What advantages and disadvantages would your suggestion have over the one proposed?

(b)   What problems can you predict for the people responsible for developing the highly compatible financial reporting system required for use on the microcomputer networks and for newly acquired units?

5   Draw up an information system set for

A car rental organization
An organization for whom you work/have worked.

Further reading

Davis, G. B., Olson, M. H., *Management Information Systems*, McGraw-Hill, 1984.

McFarlan, F. W., McKenney, J. L., Plyburn, P., *The Information Archipelago – plotting a course*, Harvard Business Review, January 1983.

Nolan, R. L., *Managing the Data Resource Function*, West 1982.

Sizer, R., Newman, P., *The Data Protection Act*, Gower, 1984.

2 Feasibility and evaluation studies

Introduction

Projects involving the use of computers vary enormously in scope and size. Sometimes special hardware or software is to be acquired. Always there is the need for the use of manpower. Some will be very big projects involving considerable sums of money – perhaps amounting to the biggest investment made by the organization concerned. But the need to make decisions on large important investments is not unique to the world of computers. Management has been involved in this process throughout commercial history. The technique of making such decisions has therefore been studied, discussed and developed continuously, and the effectiveness of decision making by computer management can only be enhanced by learning from the experience of managers in other fields. Generally there has been stress on achieving objectivity and using rational, often quantitative, techniques as the basis for decision making. The discipline is a good one and widely accepted across industry and commerce. It is also recognized however, that some important aspects of a project may prove difficult to express quantitatively with any degree of credibility, and yet they have an influence on the decision. Many aspects of a project have also an associated risk, which must somehow be assessed and included. There is also the question

of the acceptability of the proposed changes to the workforce. The conduct of the study itself and the extent to which people are affected by it are important considerations too.

There are enough issues touched on here to indicate the difficulties inherent in project assessment. Perhaps this should be no great surprise. The reduction of a decision process to a series of formulae into which figures are inserted, manipulated and a decision produced is an attractive idea, but it hardly constitutes what is generally thought of as management decision making and would not need managers to do it.

Where hardware and software acquisition specifically relates solely to the subject of one feasibility study then the evaluation process for the acquisition is bound up in that feasibility work. Often, however, equipment is acquired against a more generalized set of requirements spanning not only several different applications but also the needs of development staff for construction of systems. The techniques needed to manage this procurement have much in common with those used in feasibility studies and are therefore included at the end of the chapter to give a more comprehensive view of the decision processes of systems development management.

Organizing the study

Beginning the study

A detailed feasibility study will normally be required for each project arising from the strategic planning process (see Chapter 1). It is strategic thinking that has evolved the central idea of the project, decided on its inclusion in the application master plan, and set its priority. The key task of the feasibility study is to consider in further detail whether the application is a good one. The starting point is to examine the high level data flow diagram (e.g. Figure 1.6) which represents all the major applications systems identified within the organization. The selected application and the information flows which connect it to other applications represent the starting point for

the study. Under the microscope of a feasibility study the concept may turn out to be impractical and further work stopped. Those that go forward after the study will almost certainly be changed in some respect as a sharper focus on the project is achieved. In fact the feasibility study may be thought of as a 'second cut' in the process of defining a system. Further 'cuts' have other names (requirements study, outline design) but include similar stages – all have the same purpose of progressively refining the nature of the problem being tackled. Figure 2.1 shows the relationship between different stages in the life of a system.

The number of 'cuts' required can be increased if the complexity of the project is great. Such

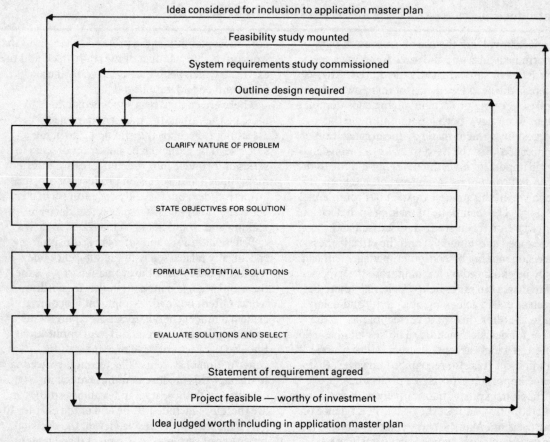

Figure 2.1   *Stages in the development of a system*

factors as size, new hardware and new users can all add to project complexity and thus increase the number of opportunities required by the system development team to study, learn and respond in their pursuit of the project's objectives. In very large projects, such as those mounted by the government, additional stages are created by pilot projects.

Terms of reference for the study
Forming terms of reference for the feasibility study is an important step in sharpening up what may be not much more than a 'wouldn't it be nice if'. . . feeling. It is likely that the steering committee or whoever directs information system development will be responsible for producing

terms of reference. One way of achieving this (recognizing that committees aren't always places where a suitable blend of creativity and precision is found) is to appoint a study team leader and have him produce terms of reference using the committee to provide guidance and to vet the results. Here is a first but crucial example of where involvement and dialogue in the management process can yield benefits. The degree of understanding and commitment to the project which the team leader will have is likely to be stronger when he has participated in preparing the guidelines for its conduct.

Matters for inclusion in a set of terms of reference for a feasibility study are to be found under the following headings.

Directives   The basic pointers for the study indicating the problem area to be tackled and its main features.

Boundaries   Specific exclusions and demarcations of system area which are to be observed.

Approach   Any special methods or products which are to be included in pursuing the study.

Conduct   The duration of the study, the budget, means of reporting and to whom.

An example of a set of terms of reference is given below.

Study title: Support for Material Control.

Purpose of study: To investigate the current means of operating material control and the likely impact of introducing a computer-based system to support it.

Direction of study: The study team should document all volumes and timings associated with the current flow of documents across the interface between the Stores Department and the Production Planning Office. The team should also forecast changes which could be achieved in this flow by the use of computer-based systems and document the expected improvements. Any solution proposed must interface with the current Stock Recording System and must not replace or disturb the existing Productivity Bonus Scheme. Proposed systems will have to be usable by shop-floor operators (currently unused to computer terminals) as well as storekeepers. Any computer terminal proposed must be capable of being demonstrated as interfacing successfully with an IBM 4300 series computer within the timescale of this study.

   The team is specifically directed to examine the appropriateness of using an MRP package for this project and is recommended to include the software products of IBM and Cincom in their study.

   A full analysis for each proposed solution is required including project costs, running costs, the timing and size of benefits and a plan of how implementation would take place highlighting any difficulties associated with acceptability to the workforce.

Organization of study: The study team is to prepare a detailed schedule based on an elapsed period of 13 weeks commencing 1/2/87. A budget of £17,500 not including seconded manpower has been provided for the study. The team will report fortnightly to the Manufacturing Director and provide interim reports to the System Steering Group as follows:

1/3/87   Verbal presentation of findings of current system

1/4/87   Verbal presentation of proposed solutions and their main features

1/5/87   Publication of final report and verbal presentation of its findings.

Team composition

The formation of a team to undertake a feasibility study is subject to the considerations which were discussed in Chapter 1. A blend of interests is required to ensure balance and objectivity. Relevant technical knowledge must also be represented. For a feasibility study the link to overall organization objectives is mainly determined by the choice of the study area and the terms of reference for that study. This means that there is a much stronger emphasis on detail than in strategic planning and less concern with external issues. The team composition will reflect this by including more middle level representatives (e.g. user section leaders, computer project leaders) than is normal for strategic work.

Style of working

A team engaged in a feasibility study has a complex technical job to perform involving the careful analysis of an existing system of people, procedures, documents and rules. If no recent improvements have been implemented in the area of the study then a degree of informality will probably exist which may make the study even harder to complete. The people working in the target area of the study are involved at several levels. First, their own jobs are to be affected. Secondly, they will have some very clear ideas about what changes are required. Thirdly, they will be able to offer some well-informed criticism of the solutions which are evolved in the study. The team is fortunate if the terms of reference for the study permit it to work in an open style and with no preconceived solution in mind. In this situation information can be collected and ideas exchanged frankly, to everyone's mutual benefit. Often, however, this is not the case and there is no sense in pretending that a study has an open brief if in fact only a narrow spectrum of solutions is to be tested. Constraints and restrictions in the study should be made clear as early as possible to those involved so that any unnecessary speculation is curtailed and effort is not expended in proposing interesting but irrelevant schemes. A good flow of communication is vital at this early stage. It is possible for individuals to have very different mental images of what is being discussed and if the study team is meticulous in recording and circulating the facts and views considered, then these misconceptions will quickly surface. In the same way tentative solutions need early and widespread distribution. Apart from the negative effect of main system users being suddenly presented with a ready-formed detailed proposal – the study team runs the risk of missing some vital objection, not visible to its members, which will invalidate their proposal.

In summary, the style of working should be one of openness and involvement. The team should air their findings and proposals as they go along, seeking as much intelligent discussion and informed criticism as they can get.

Selection of potential solutions
It is not possible to apply general rules to the formation of a set of solutions or selection of those to be studied deeply. Occasionally, a single idea is unchallenged from the very start of the study and is the only one costed. In other cases many possibilities exist and must be assessed. In this case it is normal to operate some early filtering, possibly combining the best features of several approaches to form a shortlist which should rarely exceed six alternatives. These solutions appear from various sources. Some will have their roots in current methods. Some will be inspired by seeing demonstrations or hearing about what

competitors are doing. Others may be totally novel proposals derived from a particularly creative person in the organization.

A technique sometimes used to foster this sort of inspirational creativity is that known as *brainstorming*. An informal environment is provided (e.g. a lunch session or a weekend off-site) for the parties most interested in the system proposal.

In the relaxed atmosphere which is generated, ideas start to flow. The emphasis is on concepts and not criticism. Bad ideas are allowed to die gently without embarrassing the author. Good ideas are talked through until they seem robust enough for further detailed examination. The major objective is to get people to think widely, perhaps outside everyday channels, and to avoid the trap of simply computerizing an existing manual system when more radical approaches are worthy of attention.

The set of solutions which evolves early in the study may be trimmed by some approximate analysis before detailed comparisons are necessary. Development costs which are an order of magnitude outside what is acceptable, or a wholesale change of methods likely to lead to protracted labour negotiations, or a change of major hardware supplier – all of these problems provide early negative decisions for what may otherwise be promising approaches. The remaining solutions are those which pass a series of 'acid tests':

They comply with the information system policy
They entail investment which is affordable
They seem to offer an attractive cost/benefit ratio
They are likely to be implementable and acceptable to the workforce
They can meet the demands of any essential timetable.

These solutions are then forwarded for detailed examination.

Detailed development of potential solutions
Those solutions which have passed the initial

criteria have to be sharpened into an early design with sufficient detail to enable the development project to be costed. This will help the team to learn as much about the eventual running of the proposed system as possible. As with the full design stages which come later, the biggest influence on this early design is the set of user requirements. During the feasibility study a useful way of deducing requirements and using them to shape the proposals is to formulate a series of objectives. These will provide the guidelines which allow the study team to estimate crucial factors such as staffing requirements, timetables, numbers of telecommunication lines, numbers of terminals, and amounts of disc storage. The objectives will also form the basis from which the full-scale production and installation of the application system is derived later.

Objectives can cover every facet of an application system and the project that produces it. Objectives may be concerned with timing (e.g. 'a response time of 1 second or less, for 95% of transactions'), or accuracy (e.g. 'limiting main update rejections to less than 5% of transactions'), or costs (e.g. 'at an annual running cost of not more than £15,000'), or less tangible achievements (e.g. 'ensuring that dormant customers are brought to the attention of the Area Manager on a quarterly basis').

Desirable features for any project are that it should:

- be on time
- meet budget
- meet requirements
- meet quality standards

and it should have the hallmarks of a successfully running system:

- achieve forecasted benefits
- be accepted by users
- rarely break-down
- be readily enhanced
- be secure.

Each of these desirable features can be used by the study team to generate objectives which can be discussed, modified and included.

Careful work at this stage will yield benefits during the design, building, implementation and running of the system. These objectives are a powerful means of translating the wishes of an organization's management and user departments into a blueprint for use by the system-building professionals.

Using the discipline of objective thinking the study team will have further refined each of the proposals. During this process the composition of the study team will prove to be important. Refining a proposal will involve trade-offs between conflicting objectives, e.g. extensive input validation and program development costs, ease of access to data and privacy of data, ease of system operation and security of system, guaranteed rapid terminal response time and efficient use of computer resources. The trade-offs should be made in consultation with all interested parties, rather than allowing either system development staff or users to do this work independently.

Each proposal needs to be developed to a fairly precise state. Typically, system hardware configuration diagrams will be produced, manpower use defined, timetables of operation agreed and software understood up to the point at which it is possible to make rough estimates of development costs, program sizes and run times/ response times. The feasibility study process now moves to the analysis and comparison of alternatives.

Feasibility analysis

Having operated in an entirely creative fashion in the early part of the study the team now has to employ its critical faculties to the full in order to make a thorough analysis of each proposal. The analytical criteria to be used will be understood from the terms of reference of the study. However, one inevitable concern will be for the financial implications.

Changes to costs and income

The view taken here is that there are several sets of costs to be considered.

The 'no change' cost

The cost to the organization, over a given period, of making *no* changes in the application area under consideration.

The proposal cost

The cost to the organization, over the same period, of implementing a specific proposal in the same application area.

For the sake of fair comparison of the proposals, the costs considered are those which are firm, quantifiable and substantially agreed by all members of the study team. Other changes which cannot be easily translated into costs will be looked at separately.

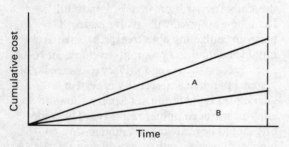

Figure 2.2   *Choosing a cost baseline*

Initially a baseline for costing must be established. For a particular application area there are many costs which could be investigated, but some of these will not vary as a result of the proposal being implemented. For example, if one considers the activities of a warehouse, costs are incurred in heating and lighting (region B in Figure 2.2) as well as labour and investment in stock (region A in Figure 2.2). For a modest proposal (e.g. changing stock-taking methods) there is no point in conducting a detailed investigation of those items included in region B when they will not change. Of course in other circumstances, (e.g. a proposal for robot retrieval systems operating from computerized picking lists) it may be necessary to look into the more fundamental items.

Once the baseline is established then all relevant detailed costs can be explored and tabulated. It is necessary to consider the phases of the development project and the period during which the application system will be running live. Within each time period a variety of costs will be incurred.

Manpower and associated costs

The salaries of the development team, the costs of special training and any recruitment needed are included under this heading, together with the salaries and associated costs of those user staff who are seconded to the project, and (if this is above the base line) those who normally work in the application area under consideration. The fees of specialists and consultants who may be brought in are also included.

Computer equipment, software and other suppliers

This includes the purchase, rental or lease cost of hardware which is or will be used in the development and running of the application; the costs of telecommunication lines and modems, terminals, concentrators and charges incurred in their installation; the cost of any use of computer bureaux for file transfer work, data preparation or the temporary running of systems; the rental or purchase of software licences and associated maintenance charges; and the costs of stationery and storage equipment, printer ribbons, tapes and discs.

Costs in the user area

Other costs associated with the project are those which are incurred in the area of application. Here it is necessary to work above the agreed baseline, ignoring overhead costs, if there is agreement that no change in them is expected as a result of any of the proposals. Typical examples of costs that may change are:

- The cost of holding stock
- The cost of financing debts
- The cost of making payments blindly (e.g. ignoring bulk or early-payment discounts offered by suppliers)
- The cost of speed of information flow (e.g.

causing manufacturing scrap by poorly communicated design changes)
- The cost of delivery and distribution (i.e. mail, transport, handling)
- The cost of using a bureau to run a service which could be handled in-house.

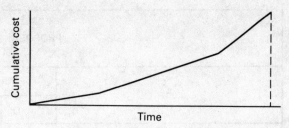

Figure 2.4 *Cost of the 'no change' approach*

Increased income
Cases where benefits are due to cost reduction have been considered but other sources of benefit exist which are based on increased income. These benefits arise because the project achieves the installation of a system which attracts a higher level of income, either on a continuing basis or for a temporary period. For example, the system may:

- Notify price changes more quickly to customers
- Enable the company to sell off equipment no longer needed
- Respond to customer queries more rapidly
- Control deadlines for contract payments.

There are powerful benefits to be obtained by attention to the income side of the business. However, agreement on the level of benefit is often difficult. A minimum figure to which all parties can subscribe should be aimed for. It is worth noting that even small percentage improvement can yield impressive benefits – a 1 per cent improvement on a sales turnover of 10 million is £100,000 per annum, which could be the total budget for a small D.P. department! Where no agreement can be reached the benefit is best excluded from these financial considerations, documented separately and brought out fully in the final discussions.

Collecting the data
Collecting together all this information requires an orderly approach. A data grid for each case should be built up (see Figure 2.3, page 38). It will be necessary to prepare one for each proposed solution and for the 'no-change' proposal.

Having this data for each solution allows the preparation of a financial profile. The 'no change' picture could be as shown in Figure 2.4. Note that

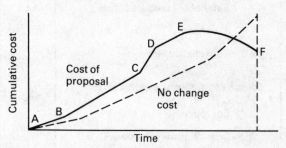

Figure 2.5 *Cost profile for a conventional project*

the cumulative cost is not steady. Surges due to cost escalation for maintaining obsolescent equipment or to the employment of extra personnel to handle an increased level of business are common.

For a proposal involving the usual development project and computer installation the profile would be as in Figure 2.5.

During AB the analysis and design work will be undertaken by a small group of analysts. Costs accelerate as programmers are added to the team (BC) and then surge when hardware costs are incurred (CD). Training and testing costs mount steadily (DE) until implementation, after which the steady realization of benefits begins to offset some of the expenditure incurred (EF). The 'no change' approach is shown as a dotted line. In this case it is seen that for the time interval considered the net cost of the proposal is ultimately less than the cost of continuing with existing methods.

Each proposal can be profiled in this way for comparative purposes (see Figure 2.6, page 39).

Operational features and acceptance
It is not easy to turn every facet of a system proposal into a precise cost or benefit to the

CASE: 'PROPOSAL X'												
Item	Year 1				Year 2				Year 3			
	Q^1	Q^2	Q^3	Q^4	Q^1	Q^2	Q^3	Q^4	Q^1	Q^2	Q^3	Q^4
Manpower costs												
Salaries + associated costs												
Expenses												
Consultancy fees												
Equipment, software, supply costs												
Computer hardware												
Communication hardware												
Software licence + maintenance												
Stationery + supplies												
Other (user) costs												
Inventory holding cost												
Cash flow costs												
TOTAL COSTS												
Benefits (user area)												
Additional income												
Second-hand value of replaced equipment												
TOTAL BENEFITS												
NET BENEFIT (COST)												

Figure 2.3   *Cost and income change grid*

company accounts. The installed system will be a complex of people, procedures and equipment. Unlike a simple piece of plant it will display unique characteristics, which may make it loved or loathed. The feasibility analysis has to explore as much of the nature of the proposed system as possible, and at the same time assess its usability and acceptability to those who work in the relevant application area. This examination of the proposal may result in the identification of substantial potential benefits. These might include:

- Tighter control of accounts
- More informed and rapid response to customers
- Sharper company image
- Better communication between departments
- Increased motivation for staff

It is possible that there has been some agreement within the study group on how these features can

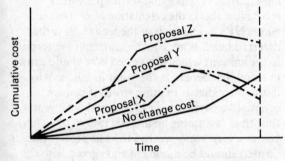

Figure 2.6   *Comparative view of cumulative costs of three proposals*

be turned into firmly forecasted cost reductions or revenue increases. If so, these features are already 'counted' in the cost profiles. If no agreement has been possible, then it is important that these claims are carefully discussed, and the means of their achievement agreed. They will then represent properly forecasted but unquantified beneficial features of the proposal. One decision required in the final stages of the feasibility analysis concerns the price which the organization is willing to pay for these features. For example, if the cost profile for Proposal A is as in Figure 2.7,

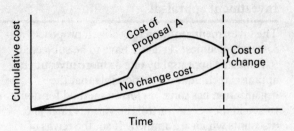

Figure 2.7   *Cost of a change to proposal A*

the cost of the change is positive and clear. This could be compared with a set of *unquantified* beneficial features which the organization is keen to have. Is this a good bargain? While techniques exist to explore the nature of the bargain (these are considered under investment appraisal), ultimately management judgement will be required in making the decision. The study team is mainly responsible for ensuring that all the desired operational features can feasibly be obtained.

Part of the team's confidence should come from exploring successfully the acceptability of the system to the workforce. The information processing role which people or groups have within organizations can often be the basis for any power or influence which they exercise. If that information processing role is disturbed (and that is what new systems do) then so is their exercise of power. Changes which appear capable of diminishing power will be resisted, and one form the resistance can take is non-acceptance of the implementation of the new system. This may be overt (e.g. mobilizing a formal trade union rejection) or more subtle (e.g. continued use of old system, unenthusiastic use of the new system, or continual criticism).

The study team should therefore consider changes to the concentration of information and to those who control it. Intelligent use of data flow diagrams can be useful in spotlighting movements of this sort. Senior management may well be prepared to meet these difficulties, perhaps by introducing compensating changes. At any event the size and scope of the problem can be charted. Office politics must not be considered irrelevant to the study. Many projects have foundered because of inadequate attention to this topic.

Investment appraisal

The investment required to realize a proposed system will almost certainly have to be subjected to a detailed appraisal by one or more investment appraisal techniques. It is possible that the organization has some preferred method for doing this, and may even control the various rates and discounts which are applied. If so, the terms of reference for the study will already contain a definition of how this phase is to be conducted.

Pay-back analysis

One of the simplest techniques is use of the *pay-back period*. This is illustrated in Figure 2.8

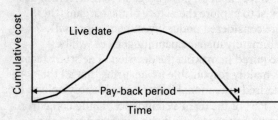

Figure 2.8   *Pay-back analysis*

The cost of the proposal has risen steadily as manpower and equipment costs mount. After the live date the benefits delivered by the system gradually compensate for the investment until at some point the investment has been recouped. The time taken to do this is known as the pay-back period. It could form the basis of a crude comparison between various proposals. However, other interesting factors such as the size of the initial outlay and the rate of benefit accrual after pay-back has been reached are not considered.

Breakeven analysis

This method is illustrated in Figure 2.9 and compares the cost profile of continuing to use the original system with that of introducing the new system. New systems usually entail significant initial investment followed by the steady accumulation of benefits which recoup that investment until at some point the cumulative cost drops below that which would be incurred if no change was made. This point is the *breakeven*

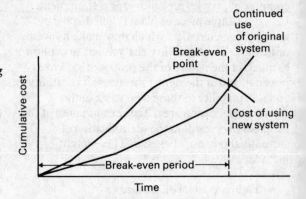

Figure 2.9   *Breakeven analysis*

point, and the period before this occurs is called the *breakeven period* or *investment period*.

Net present value

The time taken to bring in benefits (cost savings or increased income) is a crucial aspect of investment appraisal. A very popular technique which recognizes this is the calculation of *net present value* (NPV). The basis of the technique is that deferred benefits are equal in current cash terms to the amount which if invested now would grow to equal that benefit at the point in time at which it is to be realized. In other words if you are promised a payment of £11 in exactly one year's time then (assuming an interest rate of 10%) to you that is *currently* worth £10. The precise rate to be used should be discussed and agreed with the financial accountant of the organization. It is likely that the rate used will be that payable on loans held by the organization but allowances for the risk of the project or movement in interest rates may be made. Table 2.1 gives an example of how the NPV technique would be applied to a proposal. The discount factors applied in the example can be calculated from first principles. If an amount V_1 is expected one year from now, the present value of that amount (V_0) is related to V_1 by

$$V_1 = V_0(1+i)$$

where i is the assumed interest rate. Similarly, if

we expect an amount V_2, two years from now then the present value (V_0) of that is related to V_2 by

$$V_2 = V_0(1+i)(1+i)$$

Generally, for the nth year, $V_n = V_0(1+i)^n$. From our point of view the interesting relationship is $V_0 = V_n \times 1/(1+i)^n$. The factor $1/(1+i)^n$ is a discounting factor which can be applied to amounts deferred for n years in order to assess their present value.

Internal rate of return (IRR)

One way of looking at a project is to assess the *rate of return* which is achieved by implementing the proposal. If this is deduced then the proposal can be assessed against other investment opportunities available to the organization.

The *internal rate of return* (IRR) can be estimated by calculating the NPV for a set of discount rates and plotting the result (Figure 2.10, page 42, shows the results of using different rates of return for the case explored in Table 2.1). The discount rate which gives an NPV of zero (i.e. about 8 1/2% in our example) is taken as the IRR for this project.

Table 2.1 NPV calculation

	This year	Next year	2 years on	3 years on
Cost				
Hardware leasing	20,000	20,000	20,000	20,000
Software leasing	11,000	11,000	11,000	11,000
Telecoms rental	8,000	8,000	8,000	8,000
Supplies	2,000	2,000	2,000	2,000
Manpower (Development)	80,000	2,000	2,000	2,000
Manpower (User)	40,000	40,000	20,000	10,000
Total cost	161,000	83,000	63,000	53,000
Benefits				
Resale of old equipment	20,000	—	—	—
Profit on additional sales	—	50,000	130,000	200,000
Project cash flow (− VE)	(141,000)	(33,000)	67,000	147,000
Discount factors	1	.909	.826	.751
Discounted cash flow	(141,000)	(29,997)	55,342	110,397
Net present value	(5,258)			

In this calculation the costs of the various items required for the project are known. It is required to forecast the benefit over the first four years of the project, and costs are correspondingly allocated. Benefits are realized in the immediate sale of the replaced equipment (£20,000) and in the form of increased profit on sales (not expected during the first year). It is required to use a discount rate of 10% per annum.

For this proposal the NPV is negative and a strict interpretation would find against the project. However, as the adverse cashflow is relatively small it is certainly worth re-examining the values used in the calculation, and specifically it is worth re-checking that the discount rate used is the right one. Assuming that this re-appraisal changes nothing then it will be necessary to weigh this net cost against any agreed unquantifiable benefits which will be achieved by this proposal in order to determine its viability.

Discount rate used	NPV produced
6%	10,991
8%	2,579
10%	(5,258)
12%	(12,406)

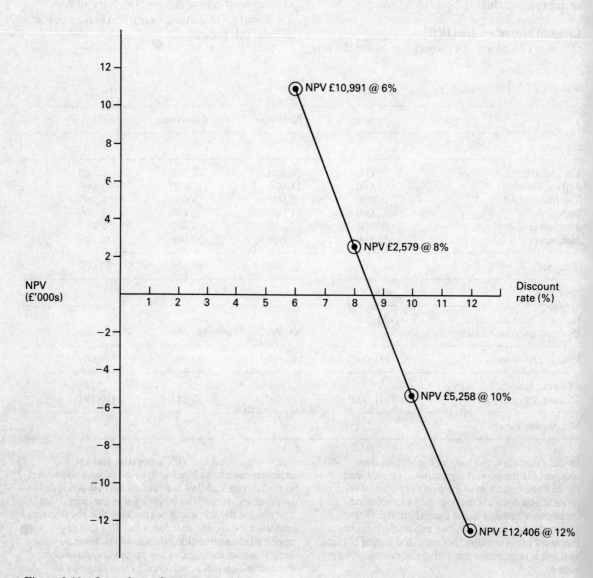

Figure 2.10   *Internal rate of return*

Investment appraisal within proposals
We have looked at some techniques which permit the quantifiable elements of a proposal to be consolidated into a handy index of one sort or another – a breakeven period, an NPV, a rate of return. We have seen that systems proposals are unlikely to be viewed in a manner which permits simple decisions to be taken. Actually, very few system proposals will emerge with clear, unchallenged net benefits. The estimation of costs, however, is a manageable exercise which, with experience and care, can be made reasonably accurate, whereas the estimation of benefits is much more contentious. It may be possible to agree that a certain proposal will deliver a benefit (e.g. permit the quotation of accurate delivery dates to customers) although impossible to agree a precise value for that benefit.

The study team must now attempt to draw together the threads of their analysis. They will, in many cases, be in the position of having to discuss proposals which show a net cost set against some unquantifiable benefits. The presentation of this comparison is important and a major objective of the feasibility report.

Feasibility reports

Structure of the report
The structure of a feasibility report has much in common with other management reports. In particular a balance must be struck between providing sufficient information to back any arguments, while not obscuring those arguments with unnecessary detail. The format of the report will vary slightly depending on the precise terms of reference. However, a useful skeleton for such reports is as follows.

1 *List of contents*

2 *Summary*
A one page précis of the whole report where the absolutely crucial issues are summarized. Written as the very last piece of the report, this section allows the writer to ensure that his main points cannot be missed by being submerged in the main body of the report.

3 *Terms of reference*
The original terms of reference for the study together with all agreed amendments and developments which have occurred during the progress of the study.

4 *Findings of the investigation*
Much of this detail can be included as appendices (e.g. current documentation, volumes of data flow, tables of any special measurements). The section should concentrate on analysis and diagnosis of the area covered by the terms of reference.

5 *Basis for change*
The objectives of the intended change should be described tracing their origins and stating any alternatives that may exist between them.

6 *Proposals*
One or more solutions which are capable of achieving the objectives described in the previous section should be covered. Passing reference to those proposals which have been discounted early should be made but most attention should be given to those which have come through for detailed examination. A sub-section describing the operation, development and implementation of each solution should be prepared. A summary of project costings should be presented for each solution.

7 *Argument and recommendations*
The possible paths forward are compared and contrasted, weighing the cost/benefit profiles against the unquantified benefits and the acceptability of the change. A set of arguments for the final selection must be laid out carefully, showing derivation from the previous analysis and consistency with the treatment of the rejected

solutions. This section is obviously a crucial one and it will be important to ensure that the study team has considered the content very carefully.

Presentation of findings
It is common practice to present verbally the contents of the feasibility study report. One approach would be to circulate the written report some days prior to the verbal presentation during which questions about the assumptions and the recommendations of the report can be asked. As stated previously a team whose report creates controversy at this stage has not been working in a sufficiently open fashion. The audience for the presentation will probably include potential system users, current system users and final decision makers – all people who should have been participating in the evolution and assessment of the proposals and who will not expect some radical new approach to be pulled out of a hat at this stage. If the work has been progressing without major controversy, and no further ideas or major doubts are generated at the presentation, then the study team leader may reasonably conclude the meeting by suggesting, to those who initially set the terms of reference, the steps which they need to take if they wish to continue to the next stage of development.

Risk assessment

The history of information system projects is sufficiently littered with disasters to ensure that a feasibility study team should realize the potential for failure which exists within the proposal they have put together. This potential needs to be analysed objectively and the analysis included in the study report for assimilation alongside the arguments for investment.

Figure 2.11 shows a list of factors which may upset the forecasted progress of a development project. Clearly if a project is based on existing equipment for an experienced user and is modest in scope then the risk element is low. By contrast, large projects with new users, entailing the acquisition of novel hardware and software, introduce substantial uncertainty. The more items from the list in Figure 2.11 which apply to a project, the larger the risk that the project will not proceed as forecasted. The right course of action, if the risk appears too large, is to revise the project to remove some of the risk factors. For example, introducing a pilot project could help to familiarize inexperienced users to new equipment. Similarly, splitting a large project into small separate projects will make the workload more manageable.

Table 2.2 Risk probabilities for non-quantified benefits

Beneficial operational feature	Possible reason for non-achievement	Probability of non-achievement
Sales staff use terminals to give up-to-date information in response to customer queries	System provides an unusable terminal response time	2%
	Slow updating renders the on-line information useless to sales staff	2%
	Office job description problem results in staff ignoring the new system	10%

DEVELOPMENT STAFF FACTORS

Large team involved

Long schedule needed

Sub-contracting needed

New skills to be acquired

USER STAFF FACTORS

Senior management commitment unknown

Users not experienced with system projects

Change in the user area is large

Several distinct user areas involved

Change to users' power position

TECHNICAL FACTORS

New main computer

New terminal devices and connecting equipment

New operating system

New language/development environment

Several equipment suppliers involved

Figure 2.11   *Factors which cause uncertainty in project proposals*

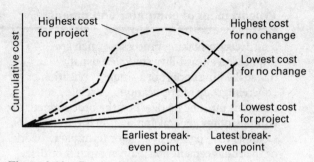

Figure 2.12   *Range of breakeven points*

Assessing the impact of imprecise forecasts involves going back to the cost and benefit assessments and applying realistic minima and maxima. This will create, for each cost or benefit, a value range which will be small for accurately known items (e.g. equipment which has been quoted) and larger for speculative items. Using these ranges it is possible to re-appraise the investment using worst and best values within the particular investment appraisal technique chosen. This will generate, for example a shortest and a longest pay-back period, or a lowest and highest NPV.

It is possible, for instance, to present a breakeven diagram showing the range of breakeven points, governed by the uncertainties inherent in the analysis. This is shown in Figure 2.12.

These assessments will enable the team to present the quantifiable side of the feasibility analysis in a way which identifies the size of the risk associated with these aspects of project. But acceptance of a proposal, as discussed earlier, is often dependent upon the unquantifiable features which will emerge after implementation. How do we express uncertainties in this key area? One way is to look at each feature and assess the probability of it being achieved. First we identify the circumstances which could impair achievement, and secondly we estimate the likelihood of these circumstances occurring. Examples are shown in Table 2.2.

The probability of non-achievement percentage is derived by synthesizing the likely failure rates of the various components of the system project which contribute to the desired feature. For example, slow updating could occur because of unexpectedly large data volumes, prolonged hardware breakdowns, poor software performance or operator mishandling. The chances of each of these occurring are assessed and combined to create the quoted 2% probability estimate. In this way the identification and assessment of risk for each non-quantified beneficial feature can be achieved. The resulting collection of probabilities will then be reported and will facilitate the decision-making process.

Procurement of computer equipment

The decision-making processes which are required in a feasibility study are usually marshalled in support of a single application or coherent group of applications. A related set of decisions must be made when the procurement of equipment for general application is required, for example the upgrade of a major terminal network, or the enhancement of a main computer or disc sub-system. In this case the team selected to control the procurement would have a stronger technical bias than the team for a typical feasibility study. However, whether the team has a general or specific brief, the procedure adopted will follow a series of steps as outlined in Figure 2.13. For minor purchases the action will be left in the hands of the management of the information system group and a reduced version of Figure 2.13 will be used.

Request for proposal

The key item in the procurement cycle is the *request for proposal* (RFP). This derives from feasibility studies or system specification documents. A key component of the RFP will be the objectives (taken or translated from these documents) which relate to the technical performance of the computer elements required in the chosen solution. These objectives should be ranked according to priority with some indication of whether they are an essential or a preferred type of objective. A list of contents for a typical RFP is shown below:

1 Background to need (extracts from the feasibility study or system specification).
2 Specification of technical requirement of proposal.
3 Indications of the format of the proposal specification required from the vendors.
4 Description of how the evaluation process will take place.
5 Timetable to be followed.
6 The vendor – general information required.

•   In the first section sufficient background concerning the purchasing organization, its

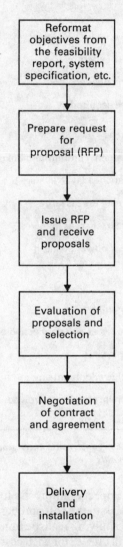

Figure 2.13   *Procurement procedure*

computing strategy and overall plan for the equipment can be outlined. The second section must contain all the critical performance targets and other desirable but less crucial attributes which the delivered equipment must have. Here, issues such as hardware availability, real-time responses, batch throughput times, delivery lead-time, engineer call-out arrangements, interfacing requirements, software standards and package compatibility are all addressed.

The third section deals with the response from the vendors and attempts to ensure some commonality between proposals. What cost figures are required? What performance details are to be quoted? What level of detail concerning operating system functions is needed? The fourth section identifies how proposals are to be judged, for example by performance trials, demonstrations, visits to current users, or detailed technical presentations. Suppliers who are forewarned will do a better job.

The fifth section gives a timetable for receipt of the proposals, the evaluation process, the decision and the expected signing of contracts.

The last section is an invitation to the vendor to provide background details about its operation; the services offered, their geographical spread, experience and organization structure.

The RFP will be delivered to a representative but manageable list of potential suppliers. Some method of filtering the total number down to no more than six should be found, otherwise the evaluation workload will be excessive. After a period of interaction during which suppliers will seek to clarify the contents of the RFP, proposals will be received and the evaluation exercise will be conducted in the form originally outlined.

Proposal evaluation

The team charged with selection from the various proposals submitted will clearly feel strongly committed to the objectives laid out in their RFP. However, an element of flexibility must now appear. Suppliers may have thought through the root problems in an unusual and attractive fashion. Conversely, none of the proposals may satisfy all the essential requirements of the RFP. In both these cases it may be necessary to issue amendments to the original RFP and seek revised proposals from *all* the suppliers.

The evaluation process will consist of several assessment steps which are discussed below.

Vendor presentations and demonstrations

Obviously a guarded and critical approach is essential during these sessions. They can be misleadingly polished and are of marginal value unless hands-on use can be arranged.

Reference visits

If a reasonably comparable group of current users can be found then much useful intelligence can be gained from them. It is best to arrange these visits oneself rather than to ask the supplier to choose what might be a favoured customer.

Benchmarks

Obtaining access to a precise example of the proposed configuration to test-run sample jobs is valuable if it can be achieved. Directly comparable configurations are notoriously hard to find. Much careful preparation for running the jobs and measuring the performance is required.

Theoretical timing

If an adequate set of base performance figures is obtained in the proposals then a skilled systems programmer will be capable of deriving theoretical times for specified batch jobs and on-line transactions. In situations where there is a narrow job-mix (e.g. a configuration dedicated to a real-time system using a small number of transaction types of known volume), the approach is simple and powerful. Where the situation is more complex it will be necessary to specify a selection of the job-mixes which could arise and then have the timings calculated. This will give a set of performance profiles which will provide a good estimate of expected performance.

Simulation

Another theoretical approach is to enlist the help of software to simulate a workload and then observe the result. A good example is the multi-user on-line test where software can create a stream of incoming messages with precise timing and transaction-mix characteristics. The generation of responses, the load imposed on the central processor and the disc activity can be monitored as the configuration responds to this simulated load. A complete set of performance figures under different loads can be obtained.

Analysis and decision phase

The evaluation process will have yielded a mass of detail which somehow has to be organized into a single selected configuration. A common technique used to do this is known as *weights and scores*. An example of how it could be applied simply is shown below.

The technique can be criticized on several grounds:

Can objectivity in setting weights or scores be achieved?

Can one objective always be traded against another?

Are weighted scores summable in this simple way?

If the final scores are very close, can there be any confidence in the supremacy of one proposal?

These criticisms are hard to discount, but there is merit in the technique, not so much because of the final answer but in the discipline engendered in the team by the derivation of the weights and scores. Objective criteria for the decision are discussed and agreed. These are then used to examine each proposal ensuring comparability of treatment. The act of weighting the objectives airs the important issues concerning which criteria are the most critical to the success of the project, and the team members are required to involve themselves in a series of crucial debates. The danger of a pivotal issue being insufficiently investigated is therefore lessened.

Weights and scores

Project: Warehouse stock movement recording and enquiry

Objectives

1 The recording system should be available between 0700-1830, 6 days per week with minimal interruption.

2 The system must ensure that movement data is collected cleanly with minimal errors being accepted at source.

3 The system must offer simple-to-use facilities for the generation of screen-based stock reports in response to selective criteria input by warehouse personnel.

4 The system must support at least 10 terminals (with further expansion being possible) offering a peak period response time within 2 seconds for 95% of transactions.

Solution A
Conventional VDU terminals are connected through a microcomputer capable of storing input data if the central mainframe is out of action.

Solution B
Uses a mixture of bar-code readers for stock recording with a smaller number of VDUs for enquiry and report purposes.

Solution C
Is similar to A but the VDUs are grouped around a minicomputer which handles all terminal interaction and deals with mainframe updates only once daily.

Score ranges for objectives

Objective 1
If system is unavailable more than 5% of required time (i.e. approx. 2 hours per working week) the rating is low.

System availability	Score
90–94%	3
95–96%	5
97–98%	8
99–100%	10

Objective 2

Accuracy of data at point of capture (read or keyed) is rated highly.

Error rate	Score
10% or more	1
5%	2
2%	7
1%	10

Objective 3

An enquiry facility which avoids jargon and provides support for naïve users scores highly.

Enquiry facility feature	Score
Formal language, training needed	4
Built-in tutor for parameter-driven approach	7
Natural language – with a help facility	10

Objective 4

Each terminal in the network is to expect a response time within 2 seconds on 95% of occasions.

Size of terminal network supported with required response	Score
10 terminals	4
12 terminals	6
15 terminals	8
20 terminals	10

Relative weight of objectives

Some objectives may be considered more attractive than others. This preference must be expressed as a weight. For example it may be that objective 1 is rated above objective 4. The judgement is that an increase in score of 4 for objective 1 would be traded against a decrease of 5 for objective 4. Similar judgements made in pairs yields weights as shown.

Objective	Weight
1	5
2	5
3	3
4	4

Objectives 1 and 2 are considered to be equal in weight, slightly more than objective 4 which in turn weighs more than objective 3.

Scoring and weighting

Each proposal is scored for its standing with respect to each objective, then the scores are weighted and summed to give a final weighted score.

Solution	Score for objective 1 ($\times$ weight=5)	Score for objective 2 ($\times$ weight=5)	Score for objective 3 ($\times$ weight=3)	Score for objective 4 ($\times$ weight=4)	Total weighted score
A	10 (50)	7 (35)	7 (21)	8 (32)	138
B	8 (40)	10 (50)	7 (21)	8 (32)	143
C	8 (40)	7 (35)	4 (12)	10 (40)	127

Solution B thus scores highest using these weights and scores. Solution A is, however, very close in total weighted score (within 5%), and this suggests that the values used in the whole process should be carefully reconsidered for accuracy and objectivity.

Exercises

1 Write four high level objectives for a project to install a network of automatic petrol dispensers which use credit card input and record transactions on cartridge tape.
2 A plant hire organization currently has two clerks using venerable visible record computer equipment for which maintenance costs are expected to grow as follows:

	This year	Next year	Year 3
Hardware maintenance costs	3600	4500	9500
Software maintenance contract	2000	4500	10 000

One solution is to buy a new minicomputer which can be delivered and installed one year from now. Hardware and software costs are £50,000 and £20,000 respectively, and initial maintenance costs are estimated at £1,000 and £1,200 for hardware and software respectively with a likely increase of 10% per annum thereafter.

Another solution can be delivered immediately, for which the costs are: hardware £60,000, software, £25,000, with maintenance of £1,500 and £1,200 respectively (again an annual 10% increase is expected).

Both solutions can be expected quickly to reduce the clerical manpower to one person. The cost of one clerk (including overheads) is £15,000 p.a., with an annual 10% increase expected.

Does either solution break even in three years? Which looks most attractive financially in that timescale? Is there any change to the financial comparison if the period of analysis is extended?
3 A major systems development activity has the following features.

During the first year a £100,000 minicomputer network is installed. Maintenance costs are expected to be £10,000 per annum initially rising to £11,000, £12,500 and £14,000 in subsequent years.

First year software development costs are £25,000 with annual software enhancement and maintenance costs estimated at £10,000, £3,000 and £5,000 thereafter.

One major benefit will be a reduction next year in inventory levels as the system reduces excess stock in the organization. Thus the spending on raw material is expected to be lowered by £150,000 for this one year.

Other benefits include an immediate (this year) one-off improvement of £5,000 due to tightened credit control, and a continuing benefit due to profit on improved sales starting next year of £20,000 with £30,000 then £35,000 each year thereafter.

Calculate the net present value for this proposal over four years using a discount rate of 10%. What is the effect of choosing to lease the minicomputer network at £3,000 per month?
4 Risk seems unavoidable for organizations moving into information systems work for the first time. Imagine you are the owner of a rapidly expanding chain of out-of-town wine warehouses. You see the value of controlling stocks and distribution using computer systems but are worried about getting it all wrong. Identify some steps you could take to minimize the risks inherent in your plans.
5 Instead of issuing a request for proposal (RFP) document, it is possible to specify fully a set of hardware and software requirements, and have each supplier simply provide a quotation against that specification (RFQ). What type of computer user or project circumstances would favour using an RFQ?

Further reading

Kleijnen, J. P. C., *Computers and Profits*, Addison Wesley, 1980.

Mumford, E., *Values Technology and Work*, Martinus Nijhoff, 1981.

Parkin, A., *Systems Management*, Arnold, 1980.

3 The organization of systems development work

Introduction

As with almost every other aspect of computing, the organization of systems development work has been greatly affected by the arrival of the microprocessor. The settled tradition of a centralized mainframe tended by a hierarchy of operators, programmers and analysts has been overturned by alternatives based on the power of distributed microcomputers. This has a wide impact on organizational issues. One fundamental change is the range of choices now available to an organization. Whereas previously the problem might simply have been to decide which of half a dozen manufacturers should supply *the* machine, now the first question is which style of computing is considered right for the organization. Only after that has been resolved will the issue of suppliers be considered. We have already seen how strategic planning takes place, but we have not considered the detailed implications which an information system strategy has for the control of the information systems development function.

The act of creating or revising this strategy should either underpin the existence of some function dedicated to information system work, or argue against it.

Who performs systems development?
In fact there is a wide variety of roles which the systems development function could take. A spectrum of alternatives is shown in Figure 3.1. Choosing a position on the spectrum is dependent on certain key characteristics of an organization.

1. The extent to which management is decentralized and unit managers are given their own profit targets.
2. The extent to which the organization has diverse aims with units setting dissimilar objectives to be achieved by dissimilar means.
3. The speed, frequency and volume of information exchange needed between different units of the organization.

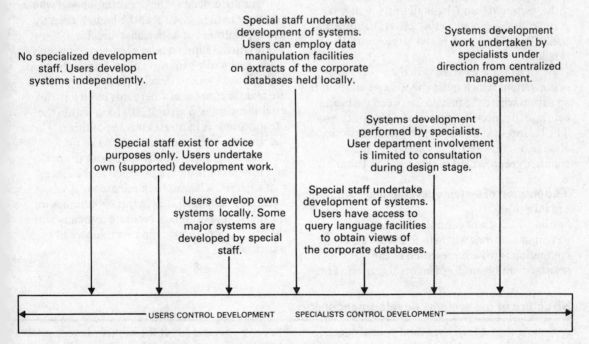

Figure 3.1   *Spectrum of control over information systems development*

Table 3.1   Control over data processing activity

Activities usually controlled by users	Disputed area. Controlled by users in de-centralized organizations. Controlled by specialists in centralized organizations	Activities controlled by centralized specialists
Setting project goals	Undertaking feasibility studies	Choosing main suppliers
Choosing input and output devices	Scheduling of processing	Devising and implementing development standards
Choosing input and output formats and timing	Choosing processing equipment for departmental use	Implementing and maintaining networks
	Undertaking development projects	

4 The understanding and competence of staff within the units to engage in tasks such as the organization and control of information system work.

Organizations which are, or are evolving towards loose federations of decentralized units, will prefer users to carry out systems development. Examples are universities, research establishments and some industrial conglomerates.

Organizations which consist of closely coupled units each undertaking relatively straightforward tasks, common throughout all units, will leave systems development to specialists. Examples are banks, building societies and large multiple retailers.

Between these extremes are the many organizations which must choose a position on the spectrum where the balance between users and centralized, specialist control is right for them. The balance will be achieved by making decisions about who controls the key activities and standards represented in column 2 of Table 3.1.

The position of systems development within the organization

Settling the issue of control over systems development work will help to decide how computing is to be represented in the management hierarchy of an organization. Three variations for this are shown in Figure 3.2.

In variation 1 the organization is highly decentralized and computing is organized to look after local needs under the guidance of the Divisional Managing Director. In variation 2 the organization has a centralized structure, and information systems are of strategic worth particularly to *one* functional area (e.g. manufacturing or finance or marketing). Computing is therefore guided by the director to whom systems matter most. In variation 3 there is a strong degree of centralization, and information systems are crucial to the organization as a whole, resulting in their control at the highest level by the appointment of a specialist director.

Variation 3 illustrates an arrangement which could lead to the evolution of an extremely strong information systems development group. There are many examples of where this has led to the establishment of a separate division within the organization. A natural extension of this is where the division begins to undertake work for outsiders (perhaps initially to smooth the peaks and troughs of in-house projects) to the extent that such work begins to dominate the division's schedules. The final step in this evolution is for the division to become a separate company within the group, or perhaps even becoming totally independent.

Structure of the systems development section

Assuming that at least a residual pool of specialists in systems development is to be retained, how are they to be organized? If the number is very small this question may be largely irrelevant. If, for

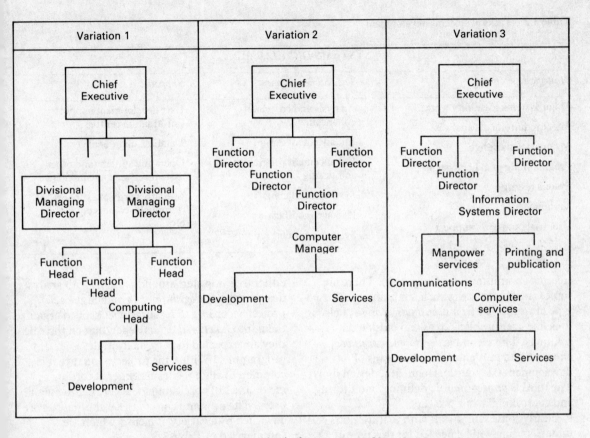

Figure 3.2   *Three variations of the position of computing in the management hierarchy of an organization*

instance, the organization approaches the fully decentralized model then there will probably be a few specialists who will simply act as internal systems consultants offering advice during feasibility studies and other key phases. Their cost may be carried as an overhead to the organization as a whole, or they may be charged out to units at a daily rate. However, most organizations of any size require a bigger investment in centralized development and therefore some structuring of the function is necessary.

Systems development tasks
Interpretations of the phrase 'systems development' may be quite varied so it is necessary to identify some of the tasks which may

be undertaken by people working in such a function. This is done in Table 3.2 (page 54). A wide interpretation has been chosen to show the full range of possibilities. In many organizations it is likely that staff involved in the tasks listed under the centre and righthand column would fall into a section called Computer Services and would not be thought of as systems development staff. However, the qualifications and training of those pursuing tasks in all three columns are likely to be very similar, and movement between them will frequently take place.

Strategic development staff exist to implement the prioritized projects identified within the application master plan, which is created and administered by those responsible for strategic planning of information systems (probably a

Table 3.2   Tasks of systems development

SYSTEMS DEVELOPMENT		
Strategic development	*Tactical development*	*Support*
Major systems feasibility work	Analysis and costing of enhancements	User development support (information centre)
Major requirements analysis		
Major systems design	Enhancement design	Database maintenance
Programming of major systems	Enhancement programming and testing	Operating system (and other system software) maintenance
System testing		
Training	System interfacing	In-house hardware support (terminals, comms equipment, etc)
User trials and early support	Package modification	
	System error correction	

steering committee – see Chapter 1). There are some crucial activities which are unique to this type of work. The first is *business analysis*, helping to define user problem areas and outline the solutions. The second is *development methods*, choosing and implementing the means of development (standards, languages, design tools). The third is *project control* , defining, monitoring and controlling major projects.

Clearly some senior staff with mature skills and understanding will be needed for this type of activity. Structuring of staff for this work can take several forms. The classic alternatives are illustrated in Figure 3.3. Essentially the choice is either to group staff around *projects*, with analysts, designers and programmers assigned to each project according to resource needs, or to organize them into *functional* teams depending on the role they are expected to play: analyst, designer or programmer. Within the project structure it is common to align the teams either according to major areas of application or according to major users. The pros and cons of these alternatives are governed by a variety of factors which are summarized in Table 3.3.

Various forms of structure exist which owe something to one or both of these alternatives. In large organizations (e.g. staff numbering more

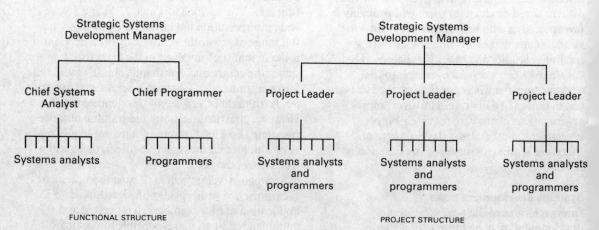

Figure 3.3   *The classic alternative structures for strategic development staff*

Table 3.3   Project vs functional structure approaches

PROJECT STRUCTURE		FUNCTIONAL STRUCTURE	
Pro	*Con*	*Pro*	*Con*
Good identification with user objectives	System documentation is largely internal to team during development and receives no public scrutiny	Individuals have a clear sense of job identity, encouraging professionalism	Responsibility for an individual project may become diffused
Promotes responsibility for deadlines/budgets		The 'airing' of the specifications between functions promotes quality	Staff are encouraged to orientate towards functions and may lose sight of organization objectives
Encourages development of specialist knowledge	Career development for individuals may be blurred by the homogenous team approach		
Tends to erode boundaries between analysis and programming jobs		Scheduling of work is simpler as there are no application specialisms to worry about	Time may be wasted in solving problems of communication between functions
	Energy may be wasted by teams competing for resources		

than about thirty) some form of project alignment is very common. To overcome the various deficiencies inherent in that choice, additional steps may be taken.

Programming pool
In this scheme only analysts, designers and other senior roles are truly project-oriented. The manpower-intensive project phases of programming and testing are achieved by temporary allocation of programmers from a pool.

Quality management
Linked to each project development stage is a quality audit undertaken by a team who work directly for the strategic systems development manager and independently assess the output of each team for the observance of installation standards, fitness for purpose, maintainability etc.

Personnel development
A system of appraisal and career development is devised and administered by a personnel specialist. This process provides the continuity of personal growth between projects which would otherwise be absent.

Tactical development staff
The implementation of a major system may mark the end of a journey for those in strategic development but it signals the start of a new responsibility for tactical development staff. Large scale live application systems are like ships. There is a constant need to correct small faults and to improve comfort and convenience. From time to time major repairs are needed, and it is likely that some extensive 're-fit' will be needed to cope with new demands. All of this type of work in the information systems field is usually referred to as *maintenance*. In addition, work other than modifying existing systems is sometimes required. A typical example is arranging interfaces between applications. This means providing some programs to permit data from one application to be used in another. Another example of a small tactical project is the modification and implementation of a small standard package where the whole job is less than a few weeks work. The criteria separating strategic from tactical development are the size and the novelty of the project, and whether the base application is live or not.

   The skills needed in tactical development are not to be thought of as inferior to those required for strategic work. It is in fact common for development managers to ensure that some of the most experienced staff are deployed in this area. The team needs to:

- Respond rapidly to faults in live systems which put the organization at risk.
- Have available a wide variety of applications experience to allow rapid assessment and implementation of enhancements.
- Be highly conversant with the live environment.
- Be committed to the provision of an efficient service to users without sacrificing the future maintainability of the systems for which they are responsible.

Support staff
The objectives of those in support are to provide and maintain various environments for users and other development staff. These environments may include those given below.

Information centre
A pool of specialists supporting user-developed systems with an emphasis on microcomputers, quick-build packages and high-level mainframe tools.

Operating system and associated software
Systems programmers receive, validate and release tailored versions of systems software enhanced with macros and other installation-specific constructs. Transaction processing monitors, sorting and general utilities as well as mainframe operating systems are handled.

Language environments
Support staff are responsible for the receipt, validation and release of compilers, code generators and associated software products, as well as the exploration of new environments. Improvement in programmer productivity is sought by the evaluation of high level tools for the rapid building of applications.

Database administration
At the heart of each application lies a database which requires definition and maintenance. Databases from separate but overlapping applications may require synchronization and databases usually require occasional reorganization. Data dictionaries, which are essential to development workers, whether they are part of the programming force using COBOL or users employing a query language, have to be built and maintained. The database administration will provide this support together with control of the software products which are used.

Communications network hardware and software
The prime responsibility for hardware maintenance, diagnosis and correction will lie with suppliers or third party maintenance dealers. However, particularly where a network is made up of several suppliers' products, there has to be support for problem solving and liaison with suppliers' engineers. This support will need to possess familiarity with communications architectures, protocols, communications software, modem and terminal test procedures. The ability to integrate a fault-finding team comprising engineers from, for example, British Telecom, modem manufacturers and terminal suppliers is essential.

Example structure
Putting together a number of the job roles discussed earlier into an example structure for a system development function achieves the result illustrated in Figure. 3.4.

Budgeting for information systems

Regardless of the means by which a systems development section secures its income, it will be required, as with any managed unit in an organization, to participate in budgeting. This

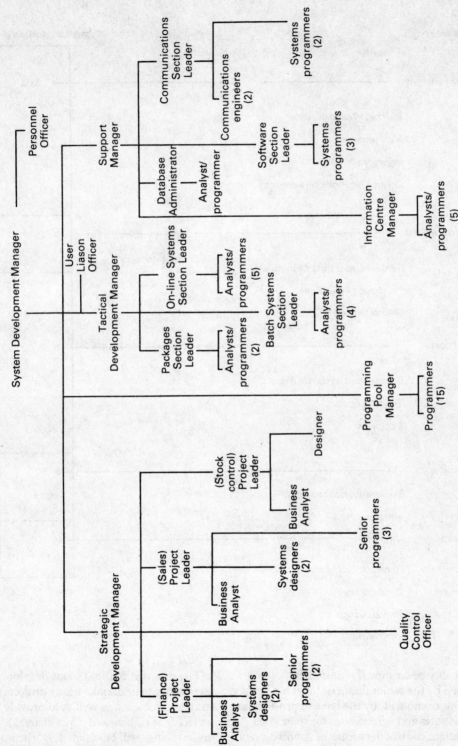

Figure 3.4　*Structure for a system development function*

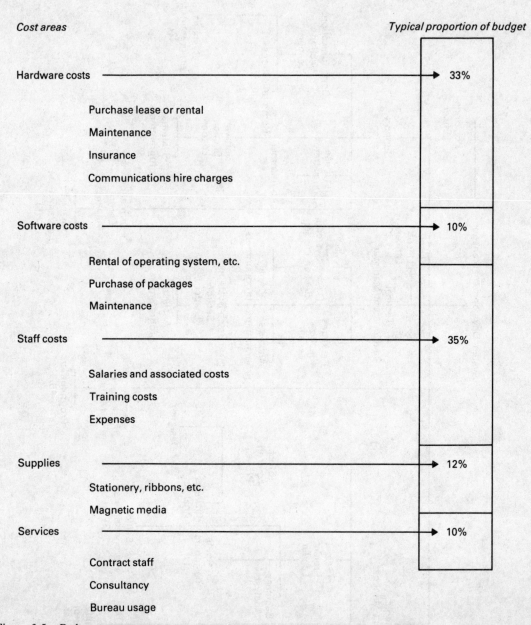

Figure 3.5   *Budget components*

will probably be an annual requirement conducted by the senior financial manager in the organization who will, by the issue of pro-formas, guidance notes and agreed rates for wage rises and inflation, control the means of submission of budgets.

The manager of the systems development section has to undertake major projects (the strategic element), as well as to provide a general service (the tactical and support areas). These undertakings will be collated, by the information systems manager, with those required to support live systems. The result will be an overall budget grouped into headings as in Figure 3.5. This will be submitted for senior management appraisal.

Negotiations for the budget

The organization's financial management will have its own concerns. The prevailing financial climate and trading forecasts for the coming year must be accommodated. This may mean that expansionist plans for the system development function are viewed sympathetically, or it may mean that economies are required. If the latter is the case then some pruning of the submitted budget will be required and, because current live running systems are usually sacrosanct, it is the systems development manager who will be required to respond. The simplest response to make is to prune the least critical projects from the schedule. Other approaches, such as promoting more user independence from support services or proliferating quicker system building methods, might also be considered. A recosting and resubmission of the budget will then take place. Further iterations and negotiations may take place until both parties have reached some defensible position.

Monitoring the budget: systems development responsibilities

If budgets have been established in this way using the categorization indicated in Figure 3.5, then monitoring of expenditure will take place along similar lines. A period budget/actual report will be made available (see Figure 3.6, page 60).

This type of report allows progress of actual expenditure against budget to be observed and, by the application of a forecasting algorithm, also projects the current trend to give future period and end-of-year analyses.

So far budgeting has been discussed in the wide context of the total information system department. However, devolution of budget control to second level managers by the head of information systems is very common and many variations of achieving this exist. One technique is to create a series of *budget centres*, e.g. operations, data control, programming, design, maintenance. Each budget centre, under the control of a manager, has a portion of the overall budget assigned to it. These portions will reflect the area in which they are being managed and could contain mainly manpower elements (e.g. design) or hardware elements (e.g. operations). Some major portions of the overall budget (e.g. planned major hardware upgrades) may be retained by the head of information systems.

Monitoring and control of budgets thus takes place at the same level as other management activities. In the case of junior managers within systems development, their actions in recruiting staff, allocating training courses and buying software aids will thus be given a financial context.

Controlling the budget

Whatever budgeting and monitoring technique is used the discipline employed is essentially the same. Those who are responsible for the day-to-day management of systems are initially required to take a detailed look at the next annual period and to negotiate and agree with senior management the resources which will be available to fulfill the objectives identified by the application master plan. Once this negotiation is complete, both parties will have a commitment to the agreement whose fulfilment will be monitored by the period reports. Within the year events will occur which can alter the consumption of resources. It is therefore essential, if the budget is to remain a meaningful control tool, that amendments to it can be negotiated. Events likely to upset the budget are numerous. The consumption of resources can be decreased, for example, by a delay in recruiting staff, or late delivery of new equipment. Increased consumption of resources can be caused by delays in removing rented equipment, unexpected price rises, or the prolonged use of contract staff.

When the period reports identify significant variances from the budget and these variances are not forecast to be absorbed during the remainder of the budget period, then either a budget amendment should be negotiated with senior management or the appropriate manager must take action which will offset the variance. In either case the budget is brought into line with the changed circumstances and will therefore continue to provide a basis for management control.

| Month | January | | | | February | | | | Mar | TOTAL | | |
	Budget	Actual/ forecast	Var.	%	Budget	Actual/ forecast	Var.	%	Budg	Budget	Actual/ forecast	Var.	%
Category									ber				
Hardware													
Main lease	8,250	8,250	0	0	8,250	/8,250	0	0		99,000	/99,000	0	0
Terminals	2,700	3,300	600	22	3,000	/3,300	300	10		42,000	/45,000	3,000	7
Comms lines	20,560	18,250	(2,310)	(11)	0	0	0	0		20,560	18,250	(2,310)	(11)
Software													
TOTAL	45,040	50,750	5,710	13	35,725	/35,500	(225)	(1)		355,600	/372,200	16,600	5

Figure 3.6   Budget monitoring output produced after recording January expenditure

Relationship of the systems development section with users

Users relate to those working on systems development at formal and informal levels. Formal level contacts are to do with the 'purchasing' of new systems, the reviewing and controlling of development projects and the 'purchasing' of enhancements and support services. Informal level contacts are through conversations, meetings, training sessions and inter-department activities of a non-technical nature.

Arguments for charging out development work

Formal relationships are effectively controlled by one important choice made within the organization: whether systems development work is to be funded from overheads or by charging project costs to the relevant user department. This choice is one which should be on the agenda of the steering committee and is really a strategic issue. The merits and pitfalls of adopting one or the other are shown in Table 3.4. Those system development sections which are set up on a charge-out basis have probably evolved to that state over a period of time. It would be unwise to establish a new development section and immediately commence a system of internal cost recovery, before that section had established any credibility.

Charging mechanisms

Charging users for system development work is usually done on the basis of the manpower and other associated resources consumed by the project.

Manpower costs

Several approaches to this are possible. One technique is to convert the salaries of individuals to an hourly rate, weighted to cover contributions to social security and pensions, together with an agreed overhead allocation. Another technique is to simply use one of a small number of standard rates, each representing the average cost of employing a certain grade of development worker.

Expense costs

Any travel, accommodation or other expenses incurred by a development worker because of his work on the project, will be charged back to the user departments.

Equipment costs

If users of live systems are already being charged for computer services in a suitably detailed fashion, then the cost incurred by development

Table 3.4 Comparison of methods for funding development projects

Development projects funded from organization overheads	Development projects funded by charging user departments
Points in favour	*Points in favour*
Easy to administer	Promotes realism in users and discourages unlikely schemes
All potential users are likely to be positive about potential systems	Involves user managers in setting priority
Priority setting effectively stays centralized in the hands of senior management	Users are more committed through the life of the development
Establishes a settled and productive atmosphere within the systems development section	Provides a means of determining the required level of system development activity and hence the size of that section

Table 3.5   Sales plan for charge-out of development

PROJECT \\ USER	January				February	
	M'power + assoc.	Expenses	Computer usage	Total	M'power + assoc.	Expenses
Transport dept. 2041	6500	550	1500	8550	6000	1000
Sales dept. 2052	500	50	—	550	1500	200

workers using computer equipment in pursuit of a user's project can be calculated by the same charging mechanism. This is a complex area and provokes many disagreements. A fair charging mechanism will count every byte of main store used, every disc sector allocated, every tape stored in the library, every line printed and CPU cycle clocked on behalf of a user. The pursuit of fairness in this way, however, probably leaves the user unable to understand what he is paying for! It may be better to use a simpler system based on, for example, elapsed time for editing, compiling and testing, which can be simply monitored and understood.

The alternative to calculating costs for the use of equipment in a development project is to arrange for an agreed portion of the total cost of the equipment used in the installation to be recovered as an overhead attached to development manpower costs.

Sales plans

Where a charge-out arrangement exists, the relationship between user departments and a system development section is that of a customer to a supplier. The supplier, in planning income for the year, will need to draw up a sales plan so that income can be projected. An example of this is shown in Table 3.5.

The basis for this sales plan is agreement on the extent of development projects, including maintenance and support work, and the likely charge-out rates.

The sales plan gives guidance on the size and distribution of income expected in the coming year. Those concerned with managing system development will wish to balance this against the equivalent budget. Arising from this comparison it is likely that some fine tuning will be required to forecast the profit or breakeven situation asked for by the organization's financial managers. The fine tuning will probably involve choosing charge-out rates to yield the required level of income. This sort of activity is precisely what any trading organization must do to achieve a profitable performance. The task could certainly benefit from the use of a computer tool (a spread-sheet package is probably adequate), but will also require good knowledge of what the 'market' will support, and careful handling of intended rate rises.

The ultimate product of this planning activity is an agreed sales plan which identifies to senior management and to user management expectations of development activity over the coming year. The budget and this sales plan together form the main basis for monitoring and control of systems development as a whole and the act of creating them is an important vehicle for bringing senior management together with management from user departments, systems development and finance in an annual restatement of the role for information systems within the organization.

Informal relationships

Every type of job in an organization has an image

associated with it. Accountants have grey suits, sombre ties and a quiet, tidy manner. Engineers have hairy jackets, protruding calculators and a voice used to rising above the noise of the shop floor. What of computing? Is there a myth to fight or prejudices to overcome? Computing as a career has been established for a relatively short time. However, some of the attitudes which non-specialists have built up with respect to computing professionals in that time are less than flattering.

One problem is jargon. Computing has quickly spawned its own vocabulary. In this it is not particularly unusual, but, because being part of a system development team means working closely with non-specialists, this vocabulary is very much on display. Being a user among a group of analysts and programmers is probably a bit like lying in a hospital bed while a team of doctors discuss which drug you should be given.

Another problem is staff turnover. Computer systems development has seen enormous growth over the last two decades and the rapid promotion of development staff is in contrast to more settled sections of the workforce. Computer staff may be seen as being loyal mainly to their own careers and never around long enough to see their ideas fully implemented.

One final area for criticism is the relative immaturity of systems development disciplines. A better understanding of the role for standards, project control, user involvement and quality control has now emerged, and estimating techniques and risk assessment are now better understood, but the computer industry has had disasters in the past. Many organizations have a history which includes defective systems and late or heavily overspent projects.

Putting these images together we have the non-specialists' view of computer staff: aloof technocrats intent on delivering systems regardless of need and heedless of users. How can we counteract this view? One way is through the establishment of formalized means of liaison. The computer steering committee is a high level example but at other levels, project review committees and design groups will all provide opportunities for computer specialists to prove that they can communicate, that they do care about quality and they are alive to what is right for the health of the organization as a whole.

A perfect opportunity for computer specialists to demonstrate their abandonment of any insularity is provided by their attitude to implementing a strategy for decentralized computing. Where such a strategy is agreed it can be assumed that most users will be energetic in their pursuit of the necessary resources. The specialists who are reluctant in their support for this initiative risk frustrating an important strategic goal and defining for themselves a decreasing role, concerned only with the rump of centralized work. Those who are, by contrast, active in supporting users and keen to pass on their experience will participate in the continually widening circle of information systems which becomes possible with each new technological development. This growth of the support role is a key development for the computer specialist and, technical skills aside, the role makes heavy demands on the communicating ability of that specialist. So it seems that the very attribute for which the computing profession has been criticized is the cornerstone of its future position! The implications for college courses and in-career training are obvious. Most computer staff must now expect to have their written and spoken skills brought up to acceptable standards by explicit training for inter-personal communications.

Systems development frameworks

Finding problems

Early efforts to produce computer-based systems do not merit the term 'system development'. A technique of the sort illustrated in Figure 3.7 (page 64) would probably have been used.

This is not a satisfactory method of developing

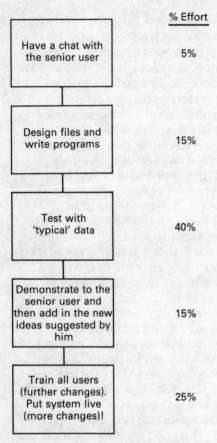

	% Effort
Have a chat with the senior user	5%
Design files and write programs	15%
Test with 'typical' data	40%
Demonstrate to the senior user and then add in the new ideas suggested by him	15%
Train all users (further changes). Put system live (more changes)!	25%

Figure 3.7   *Early development approach*

systems. If one considers the chain of events listed in Figure 3.7, three main issues emerge.

User involvement
The role of users in the process as illustrated is somehow to deliver, in a series of unstructured conversations, a specification of their requirements which is accurate, complete and unchanging. No further involvement is expected.

Design vs production
The race to begin coding results in skimped analysis and design. Design errors are then corrected by programming changes. Those spotted by the user during training are corrected by even later programming changes. The testing and training phases are therefore extensive and fraught.

Manageability
The lack of structure means that projects slide from stage to stage. Without a definition of the output expected from a stage there is difficulty in determining whether or not that stage has been completed. Managing for quality, timeliness or cost is thus made very difficult.

Much effort has gone into improving the development process by attending to these three areas, in the following ways.

Increased user involvement
This has been sought in a variety of ways, such as the production of a formal user requirement specification, the encouragement of user participation in design committees, the prototyping of the intended system in conjunction with users, and the definition of formal acceptance trials.

Better analysis and design
Separation of the design process into several discrete tasks is carried out. Each task is clearly defined and its achievement marked by the production of a standardized output which is used as input to later tasks. Various practitioners have defined and linked tasks together in a distinctive style which they then refer to as their methodology.

Management by structure
The breaking down of development projects into phases is a great help to project managers. Each phase will have its completion formally identified by a set of outputs. Future estimates of project duration and costs can thus be based on accurate views of the progress of previous projects. Quality can be monitored by review of the outputs themselves.

The life cycle of systems: phases and loops
System developers have gradually evolved an approach to their work which is known as the *systems life cycle*. The main phases and outputs are described in Table 3.6. Why a cycle? At the end of the last phase is the hint that the process will repeat itself at some later stage, when events have overtaken the effectiveness of the system.

The ordered simplicity of the system life cycle is attractive, and it would be pleasant to report that the approach has brought peace and certainty to the field of software development. However, this is not the case and, although better definition and management is evolving on the basis of the life cycle, several problems remain intractable.

Table 3.6   Systems life cycle

Main phases	Main outputs
Feasibility phase	Outline objectives Outline solution Plan for next phase
Requirements analysis phase	Information model Performance requirements Plan for next phase
Logical design phase	I/O design Data model Functional design Plan for next phase
Physical design phase	Data base specification Transaction specifications Program structures Plan for next phase
System construction phase	Tested programs Integrated systems Operating documentation Implementation plan
Implementation phase	Acceptance trials completed Users trained Data taken-on System running live
Post implementation phase	System enhancements Audit reports Recommendation for replacement?

Establishment of requirements
It is almost certainly naïve to expect users either to know in detail or to understand the implications of their requirements in the context of a computer-based system.

Communication between users and developers
These groups have different work patterns, jargon and motivation. Verbal and written communication between them is prone to misunderstanding.

Successful linking of the life cycle phases
While each phase can be defined in terms of its end product, what is often not so certain is how those working on the next phase should use that output. For example, how does a statement of requirement transform into a design specification?

Focus on development methods
These problems have been tackled by various people including D.P. practitioners, academics, authors and consultants, each proposing solutions which address some part of the system life cycle. The work done is based on three main standpoints as shown in Figure 3.8 (page 66).

The human focus
Those working from this standpoint recognize that the computer will form only one element of the finally implemented system, and they lay particular emphasis on the role which users should have in the development process. The *human activity system* approach would be taken right at the outset of a project. It is concerned with establishing a clear understanding of the zone in which the system is to be implemented. A broad view must be taken, by finding out about the social and political climate, the identity of the participants and their different objectives, and the objects and messages which exist and flow. The results should be understood and charted. One major outcome could be a redefinition of what was thought to be the original problem. An essential feature of this approach is that new systems are not devised until the old one is fully analysed.

Prototyping is dealt with separately in the next section. Essentially this method telescopes the whole system life cycle into a short, relatively unstructured process with close user involvement. This process is then repeated a number of times until the user finds the final system acceptable.

Socio-technical design emphasizes the role for the real users of the system (e.g. accounts clerks,

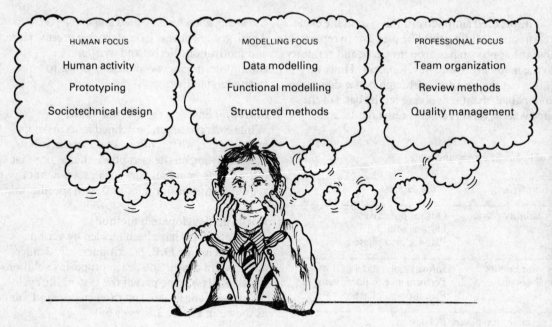

Figure 3.8   *Three standpoints in the evolution of system development*

and not just the chief accountant) in the design of their system. The vehicle for this participative process is often a committee or design group made up from those most closely involved in the system change. Clearly a committee of this complexion is capable of weighing up issues of social interaction and job content as well as technical aspects of the proposed system. Progress is made by progressive refinement of a number of social and technical alternatives until, judged by its ranking against agreed criteria (costs, disruption, benefits etc.) a preferred combination emerges.

The modelling focus
Techniques grouped under this category give developers sets of symbols, rules and forms of documentation with which to proceed. They thus give valuable guidance on how to move from the beginning of a phase to the end. Each technique tends to concentrate on some portion or portions of the development process. *Data analysis* is used to explore the relationship between objects in the user world and will lead to decisions about how data will be stored. *Entity life cycle analysis* models the events which impact an object in the user

world and thus analyses the need for transactions. *Functional analysis* is used to examine the procedural side of systems, breaking down (decomposing) a user's functional responsibilities until a full description of procedures is obtained. The boundary between human procedures and computer procedures can then be chosen.

The techniques grouped under the modelling focus act as a discipline (like using an intelligent checklist) to ensure that all the right questions are asked, that answers are unambiguously recorded and that each situation is fully explored. Examples of some of the better known 'brand name' methodologies are listed in Table 3.7.

The professional focus
Some effort has been concentrated in the organization of the development team itself – to find ways to use developers as effectively as possible. *The chief programmer team* is a form of organization whereby several teams are created each headed by a 'chief'. Supporting roles are defined for all team members except this 'chief'. The concept is similar to a legal defence team with the Q.C. at the head backed by junior counsel,

Table 3.7 Some system development methodologies

Identity	Comments
Human activity systems (Associated with Checkland)	Explores the problem area thoroughly before any design is undertaken
Socio-technical design (Associated with Land and Mumford)	Ensures balance by incorporating users fully in the design process
ISAC (Associated with Lundeberg)	Looks carefully at changes of user procedure, and documents future user activity as well as the intended information system
Information engineering (Associated with Palmer, McDonald and James Martin)	Derives from a data analysis approach, this methodology also describes process analysis and includes a strategic planning element
Structured analysis and structured design (Associated with Gane and Sarson, Yourdon)	The main analytic techniques are the documentation of data flow, the use of structured English to describe detailed procedures and data analysis by normalization
Jackson system development (JSD) (Associated with Michael Jackson)	Focuses on the flow of events by modelling the life of major entities. Subsequent steps add in the desired user functions and decide on the structure of processes
Structured systems analysis and design methodology (SSADM) (Learmonth and Burchett)	Primarily a data-driven approach, this methodology also incorporates data flow techniques and analysis of entity events

solicitors and secretaries. *Structured walkthroughs* are used to bring the experience of a group of people to bear on the products of perhaps just one of their number. The design or coded outputs of this individual are presented by him to a group of fellow workers who brainstorm the work, thus providing insight to potential problem areas. *Quality control*, an approach borrowed from other professions, sets out to ensure integrity of the constructed system by staged objective reviews conducted by authorities other than those who have performed the construction. Clearly the quality control function is dependent upon fully accepted standards for development, and well-defined end points for each task.

The prototyping approach

Most people would probably not want to get involved in designing an electric toaster. They are perfectly happy to look at the options available and choose one. Any attempt to design one themselves or even instruct a designer, might result in difficulties or inadequacies.

Similarly, in the development of computer systems, we can imagine the problem which a user has in specifying requirements. It would be easier if the user could simply look at an actual system and say what is good and what is unacceptable.

The development technique known as prototyping is a response to this idea. After a minimum of discussion with a user, the designer goes away and produces a prototype of the required system. This prototype is not expected to survive for very long. During its demonstration the user will correct the designer's misconceptions, discover his own unstated assumptions and may also be prodded into new and creative thoughts. This generates a further prototype and further demonstrations and discussions take place. The process may continue until one of two desired end points is reached. This is shown in Figure 3.9 for a three prototype process. The refined prototype may be acceptable as the finished application system. However, in many cases, while the final prototype may fulfill all the user's logical requirements it may be deficient in several other respects:

Performance may be poor, particularly response times for data retrieval.
Security and privacy may have been entirely neglected.
Interfacing to existing systems may be impossible with the prototype.
Maintenance may be difficult because of inadequate use of standards.

In this case it will be necessary to treat the prototype development process as a means of obtaining a statement of requirement for a user. Conventional design steps can then be taken in the knowledge that requirements are thoroughly researched and understood.

Prototyping can only work economically if versions can be built quickly. The method thus depends on the availability of quick-build tools. An early prototype (illustrating I/O features) may be achieved with nothing more than a screen design facility. For later versions a non-procedural language using relational database facilities is useful. The designer can maintain and enhance conventional systems documentation (e.g. data dictionaries and program structures) in parallel with his development of the prototypes, and this will facilitate future support and maintenance work if the final prototype is made operational.

The application of prototyping has been discussed with an implicit image of two people in partnership – the user and the designer. Many small systems conform to this image and the role for prototyping looks clear in that context. However, some application systems have other characteristics: they may span several departments in an organization, they may be used interactively by many users, and they may require several designers to contribute to their development. Clearly for such applications there is little likelihood that a final prototype could ever become the live application. However, the method still has some validity if it is scheduled carefully into the initial stages of requirements analysis. The key feature of the method, the opportunity for the user to contribute to establishing requirements by choosing, reacting and responding to visible suggestions rather than creating ideas in a vacuum, is valuable and will find a place in many large-scale projects.

Choice of development methods

The choice of system development methods available to managers is wide and confusing. Some appear to span the whole development cycle, others have obvious application in just a narrow portion of it. Some methods require precise techniques to be learnt and applied, others are more like codes of conduct that urge that appropriate attitudes be adopted. An attempt to summarize the applicability of the methods previously represented in Figure 3.8 is made in Table 3.8 (page 70). The only method which seems to span the cycle completely is prototyping

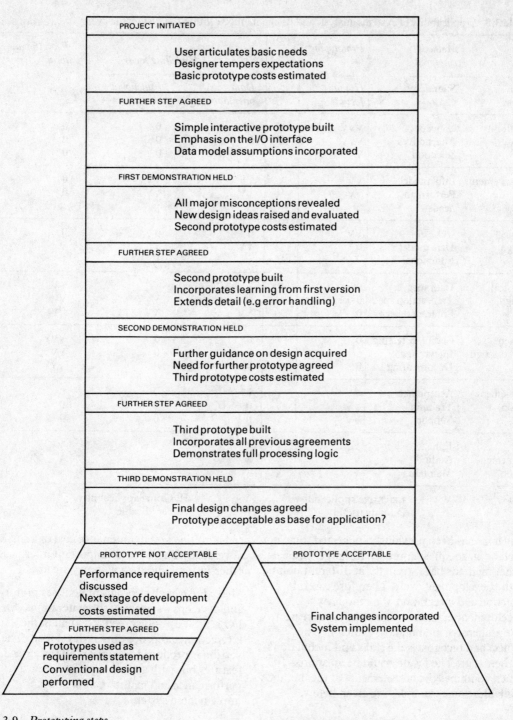

Figure 3.9 *Prototyping steps*

Table 3.8 Applicability of systems analysis and design methods within the system life cycle

Main phase	Subsidiary phase	Prototyping		Modelling focus		Professional focus
		Human focus		Data orientation	Functional orientation	
Feasibility	Concept	√√√	√	0	0	0
	Alternatives	√√√	√	0	0	0
	Selection	√√√	√	0	0	0
Requirements analysis	Info' model	√√	√	√√√	√√√	0
	Performance needs	√√	√	√√	√√	0
Logical design	I/O	√√	√	0	0	0
	Data model	√	√	√√√	√	√
	Functional	√	√	√	√√√	√
Physical design	Data spec	0	√	√√√	√	√√
	Transaction spec.	0	√	√	√√√	√√
	Program design	0	√	√√	√√	√√√
System construction	Coding & testing	0	√	0	0	√√√
	Integrating	0	√	0	0	√√√
	Documenting	0	√	0	0	√√√
Implementation	Acceptance	√√	√	0	0	0
	Training	√√	√	0	0	0
	Support	√√	√	0	0	0
Post-implementation	Enhance	√	√	√√	√√	√√
	Audit	√	√	√	√	√
	Maintain	√	√	√	√	√

Key	√√√	Extensive applicability	√√	Has some applicability
	√	Possibly useful	0	Not applicable

which, as has been previously suggested, may not itself be an adequate approach for larger projects. Other methods have strengths at different points in the development cycle. Therefore careful selection and integration of methods by development managers is necessary, to create a comprehensive methodology which fits the project and recognizes the skills and inclinations of their staff. The result would be an approach which combines the best elements of the methods available. Some examples are given below.

Requirement: A transport manager requires an information system to monitor the age, fuel consumption and maintenance cost of a small fleet of vehicles. There are no important interfaces to other systems and data volumes are low.

Method: An analyst/programmer uses prototyping and develops a system in three iterations. First the I/O is built up and agreed. Next all of the interaction and processing is developed. The final version is produced to support all the agreed features but with attention paid to security, performance and maintainability of the implemented system.

Requirement: A sales forecasting module is to be developed which will be based upon an existing sales order processing system. A small number of key personnel in sales, customer service and stock control departments are affected.

Method: The system concept is initially explored using a human activity system approach. Requirements are then built up with the help of data modelling and by using prototyping for the I/O design. Reviews of the results are conducted by a group which includes all the key users who ultimately select the features they require and are responsible for the production of a requirements statement with the help of a development project leader. Detailed design and specification takes place under the direction of this project leader using a team of two analyst/programmers who continue to use a data modelling method but also develop transaction sets with the help of entity life cycle analysis. Structured program designs are reviewed by walkthroughs as are the preliminary program and system test results. The user review group designs and undertakes an additional level of testing prior to implementation.

Requirement: A fully integrated accountng system is to be implemented across an organization in response to the genuine concern about the current system expressed by a new financial director. Apart from the accounts department, the purchase control and customer service departments are deeply affected. All other departments are involved to a lesser but significant degree.

Method: A steering group of departmental managers work with a development project manager to examine the system concept. Analysis of the human activity systems helps to define the boundaries, identify conflicts of interest and sharpen up the objectives. A design sub-committee is commissioned to produce an initial prototype which succeeds in identifying several anomalies in the proposed account coding structure. A second prototype concentrates on I/O and is able to assist decisions about the interface for terminal users. A statement of requirements is published by the steering group.

The project manager leads a team of four analysts in the detailed analysis and design for the system using a combination of data and functionally-oriented techniques (e.g. Learmonth and Burchett's SSADM). Anomalies which evolve during this stage are demonstrated to the steering group, often with the help of the prototypes developed earlier, and resolved. A design specification is published.

The project team is now expanded to include ten programmers and split into groups of three (including a group leader) each with responsibility for a particular component of the total system. In addition a quality controller attends all reviews and walkthroughs and acts as assistant to the project manager. The steering group continues to meet regularly and the project manager arranges for the viewing and demonstration of partial results as well as supplying project control information. A schedule of training, formal acceptance trials and support manning is drawn up to run during the take-on of data, parallel running and first few weeks of live running. The steering group continues to have less regular meetings to monitor the system, commission audits and agree adaptations and enhancements.

Exercises

1 A crucial board meeting of MultiCo UK is being held at which the future of the computer division is to be decided. Some directors are in favour of encouraging the computer division to tender for non-company work. Others wish to dedicate the division to the needs of MultiCo UK. Identify some of the arguments you would expect to hear from each side.

2 Using the structure in Figure 3.4 identify how the following situations would be dealt with.
  a) a consultancy wishes to 'present' (i.e. to sell) a microcomputer-based tool intended to assist the particular design method currently in use. How would you propose that the consultant and his product are handled?
  b) A small independent organization has been

purchased by a larger company as a means of diversifying. The systems development manager of the parent company wishes to take three of his staff for an initial meeting with the senior management of the new unit to assess the status quo and discuss future plans. Who should he take and why?

3 As a systems development manager do you think your task of budgeting would be easier or more difficult if you devolve most of your portion of the overall budget to your subordinates?

Using Figure 3.4 identify the budget centres which you would declare, giving reasons for your choice.

4 Prototyping could easily encourage slipshod methods in development projects. How would you encourage the use of prototyping while protecting against that danger?

5 Recently appointed to a position as a systems development manager you have decided to implement development standards for your analyst/designers based on a popular methodology. List separately the arguments you would use to convince the following people that your decision makes sense: the head of information services, the analysts and designers, and a group of user managers.

Further reading

Lundeberg, M., Goldkuhl, G., Nilsson, A., *Information Systems Development*, Prentice-Hall, 1981.

Maddison, R. N., *Information System Methodologies*, Heydon, 1983.

Nolan, R. L., *Managing the Data Resource Function*, West 1982.

Wood Harper, A. T., Antill, L., Avison, D. E., *Information Systems Definition: The Multiview Approach*, Blackwell Scientific Publications, 1985.

4 Project planning

Introduction

Previous chapters have been concerned with planning and management at elevated levels (strategic or departmental), and have considered the evolution of a system from the initial concepts to one which has form, is considered feasible and is selected for investment. This chapter, and the two that follow, are concerned largely with the progress of systems development projects as they are managed by project leaders and project managers within the data processing function. The task is akin to project management in any sphere of working life and has much in common with contract manufacturing, civil engineering or ship-building. Common themes are timescales, budgets, contingencies, communication and the black art of work estimation.

The resource being managed in data processing projects is principally the human one, although of course equipment deliveries and computer usage can be very important. One difficulty arises from the way that projects progressively go *underground*, that is to say, become distanced from the users. User involvement is, quite correctly, extensive during the feasibility and requirements analysis phases of a project, but during the later stages of design and construction a role for users is harder to define. It is the responsibility of the project manager to combat any tendency for users to lose contact with the project team during these phases. The use of prototyping, either as an aid to requirements exploration or as the main development method, helps maintain user involvement. If however, prototyping is not formally chosen as part of the overall method then other methods should be used to ensure that contact is maintained. Reviews, for example, present opportunities for user involvement, and every care should be taken to make these sessions as informative as possible.

Why plan?

One of the important principles of planning and controlling projects is recognizing the need for continuous re-assessment and adjustment of the plan. If the plan is always changing, what use is it? There are many advantages in conceiving and using planning information. Some are to do with motivational objectives, which are considered in Chapter 6. Others arise from the ability to recognize and respond to disturbances. These are considered in Chapter 5. The advantages we consider in this chapter are concerned with the clarification which detailed planning provides for those devising the project. Successful planning will tease out the complexity of an undertaking and will create documentation detailing all the intended tasks to be handled.

Creating a fully detailed plan of a future project is an attractive but difficult objective. Look back over a collection of systems development projects and study the catalogue of events and disturbances that occurred within each one. The catalogue will contain scores of interesting items – some minor, some momentous, some bizarre. In planning a new project the planner is being asked to invent a world that contains just such a rich pattern. It is an act of creation comparable with writing a film script or a novel. In fact it is perhaps more difficult because the planner is required to have his creation measured against actual events while the script writer is liable to no such assessment.

Planning systems development projects is therefore a difficult and imaginative task, like many other management tasks. That difficulty is evidenced by the history of failures to which poor planning has made its contribution. Overspent budgets, overrun timescales, systems that are poor in quality or fail to deliver benefits – all illustrate the effect of poor planning. Some reasons for these past failures are shown in Table 4.1.

Table 4.1 attempts to discriminate between planning mistakes and other types of difficulty which can cause project failure. The discrimination may appear arbitrary but a tendency to blame poor planning for almost all failures should be resisted. Planning is only part of the total process.

In fact Figure 4.1 shows the relationship between *planning* and the other processes of

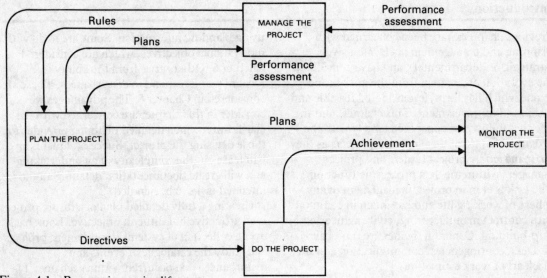

Figure 4.1   *Processes in a project life*

managing, monitoring and doing. It should be clear that poor performance in a project can arise because of difficulties in each of these other processes.

Table 4.1   Causes of project failure

Planning mistakes	Other types of difficulty
List of tasks incomplete	Equipment deficiencies
Task estimates too low	Staff not adequately capable
Interdependence of tasks not noted	No user commitment
	Poor use of standards
Insufficient contingency used	No effective methodology in use
Effect of staff turnover ignored	Outputs of planning and monitoring not acted upon
Planning not reviewed adequately	

Planning overview

Phase planning
A significant system development project may be established and re-established several times over as further investment decisions are taken. At each point some resource is committed after an appraisal of costs, benefits and risks. The team size may be adjusted, or a wholesale change of personnel may take place. At each break point there can be detailed planning for activities leading to the *next* break point, in the light of the understanding obtained from the preceding work.

Between each break point is a *phase*. Each of these phases represents a period during which different circumstances prevail. Phases may differ in the level of management commitment, the number and type of personnel involved, the work being done or its pace and urgency. Thus the project planning, monitoring and controlling required may change from phase to phase. As the project develops, phases tend to become more susceptible to analysis by *task breakdown*. During the construction phase for example, it is possible to

PHASE	ACTIVITY	TYPICAL TEAM MAKE-UP	PLANNING BASIS
Concept	Discuss ideas	Users and one practitioner	None
Decision : Is concept worthwhile exploring?			
Feasibility	Statement of problem Proposal of solutions Analysis of solutions	Mixed group of users and practitioners	Global estimates
Decision : Is solution feasible and beneficial?			
Requirements analysis and system design	Detailed models of existing and proposed systems prepared Specification of system completed	User advisory group with several practitioners committed	Task breakdown based on the methodology employed
Decision : Can the system be constructed within budget?			
Construction of system	Write and generate programs Integrate and test system	Many practitioners involved Users participate in review groups	Task breakdown based on modules of construction (program, document, etc.)
Decision : Is system fit for publication?			
Implementation	Train users Take-on data Support live use	Users with practitioners in support	Global estimates

Figure 4.2   *Phases and their characteristics*

think of individual tasks being completed and integrated into the total system. Traditionally, this approach has been less obviously applicable in earlier phases where investigative work is usually conducted within a looser format. One effect of choosing and using an analysis and design methodology will be to formalize these investigative phases according to the types of output which the methodology requires (e.g. data flow diagrams, entity life cycles, entity-relationship models). In this way planning for these phases can be approached as systematically as for the construction phase, with a consequent improvement in planning and control. Some revision to the planning of earlier phases must be expected, and this should not be seen as

necessarily indicating poor previous work. We need not, for example, go back and rerun the feasibility phase just because the design phase has discovered the need for an extra disc drive to be on-line. It *does* mean that the project manager must check that the cost-benefit balance is not significantly altered by an extra need, and he must ensure that principal parties are aware of the alteration.

Figure 4.2 illustrates the relationship between different project phases and their characteristics.

Apart from prototyping, which is fully discussed as a sole development method in the previous chapter, all other combinations of methods result in key outputs being delivered within a particular phase. When a complete set of outputs is available they will be reviewed and the phase deemed complete. The relationship of outputs to phases is shown in Table. 4.2.

Table 4.2   Outputs of the phases of systems development

Phase	Outputs of the phase including planning forms
Feasibility	Feasibility report. Overall plan. Detailed plan for the next phase. Pointers for project methods, planning and management style. Budget.
Analysis of requirement	Statement of user's requirements. Amended overall plan. Detailed plan for next phase. Revised budget.
Design and specification	Outline design specification. Program specification. Data storage specification. Manual procedures. Testing objectives. Detailed plan for the next phase. Revised budget.
Construction and testing	Tested system. Documentation for maintenance, operations and users. Detailed plan for next phase. Revised budget.
Implementation	Accepted system in use.

Global estimates

In the early stages of a project's life it is necessary to estimate the timescale and the expected consumption of resources. This is not simply to serve financial considerations: some systems development managers deliberately plan to keep projects below a certain size and duration, e.g. not more than three man-years or one calendar year for completion. The 'small is beautiful' ethos is the result of experience of long projects which are often beset by changes in the environment in which they exist, and by the volume of communication between participants needed in large project teams. Disturbances include events like:

Development staff leaving the organization
New recruits being absorbed
Turnover of user department staff
Changes in user expectations
Subtle shifts of organization policy
Hardware and software becoming obsolescent.

The longer the project, the more likely it is that some of these events will affect the planning, and hence the smooth control of the project.

Communication between participants is a problem related to project size. If a project involves n people (including development staff and key users) then $n(n-1)/2$ lines of communication are needed between them. Problems often arise because of 'noise' on such lines of communication (e.g. a user misunderstands a jargon word). Thus the number of problems will rise steeply with the number of participants. A five person project requires ten lines of communication while a ten person project needs 45.

It therefore appears to be in the interests of systems development managers to keep projects small and quick, although of course problems and solutions do not fall conveniently into handy units. Devotees of the small approach will respond by chopping large projects into several smaller ones. However, the difficulty is then to make each of these projects worthwhile in the sense of having the type of independent justification and benefits which are meaningful and acceptable to the key users.

Large or small, there will be a requirement to produce global project estimates. In this, the record of the software development industry is appalling. Error factors of 200% or 300% are not uncommon and worse figures are known. Two approaches to the problem are most popular: use of previous records and use of formulae. Of the two, the former is the most widespread and, as the industry becomes more mature, has the potential for increasing accuracy.

The difficulties lie in assessing comparability of the current project with those in the records. So many factors can compromise that comparability: for example differences in the problems, personnel, hardware and software. In allowing for these differences the project estimator will guard against excessive optimism. A previous project will have had unpredictable disturbances which, although they may not occur again, may be replaced by as yet unimagined problems for the current project.

The use of formulae depends most heavily on the assessment of the number of lines of code expected for the system. In a survey by Johnson (see *Further reading*), sixteen commercial data processing projects were examined. Five small projects (i.e. less than a man-year) produced figures for lines of code per man-day which varied between 54 and 100 with an average of 70. Eleven larger projects (between 1½ and 200 man-years) produced corresponding figures which varied between 9 and 45 with an average of 23. Thus selecting a base rate for lines of code per man-day must be influenced by a subjective assessment of the eventual size of the project. Another factor which will tend to depress the figure is the novelty of key aspects of the project: is this a first-time user; a first use of DBMS; a first micro-mainframe link?

Having selected a base rate, the estimator has then to estimate the number of batch and on-line programs required and their size. This yields a total figure for lines of code and, by use of the base rate, an estimate of the man-hours required. It would be useful for the estimator to use both the formulae and previous records methods and attempt to reconcile any differences by re-examining the assumptions that have led to the incompatability.

Clearly the act of creating these global estimates is hard to get right. The estimator ought to document the methods and assumptions used in creating the estimates, and to circulate a discussion document to a broad spectrum of users, designers and programmers to ensure that no obvious component of the project has been omitted. These global estimates are the basis for project cost forecasts and future detailed planning, and therefore an understanding of them and their derivation is an important step in obtaining a broad commitment to the project in its early stages.

Resource issues

Part of the higher level planning activity undertaken for a system development project is the consideration of a resource strategy. Before detailed estimates can be made and tasks scheduled, resources have to be chosen to suit the cost estimates, timescale and in-house skills which currently exist. The feasibility study team will have made some of these choices, but others will be made during analysis and design, or will emerge as tactical expedients in later phases.

Assessment of in-house skills
A key step is a realistic assessment of what skills currently exist within the organization. These must be compared with the skills which the project requires, and if a gap is identified then the resource strategy must include details of how that gap will be closed. One area likely to suffer from skill deficiency is the feasibility study itself.

Mature, impartial judgement and experience of several complete systems development projects are the best foundation for leading a feasibility study. If the organization does not have individuals with this background then recruitment, or the use of consultants, should be considered. Similarly, the skills of project management are essential to the success of sizeable projects and individuals with those skills must be identified and appointed to the project early. In neither of the above cases is it likely that formal training will be sufficient to make good the deficiency. In other cases, however, a training course may well be the solution to the problem. Where new development methods, software or hardware products are to be used then a timely course will be helpful – although some allowance for unfamiliarity with the product or method will be required when estimates are being made.

Where skill assessment identifies major shortfalls across the company then serious consideration should be given as to the viability of the project. Alternatives are to sub-contract the complete project to an external agency (discussed later in this section), or to defer the project until in-house development staff are better experienced.

Assessment of human resource levels

Where outline estimates indicate a need for more human resources than currently exist within the systems development section then action is needed. The options are to sub-contract, for example, the programming work to a computer services company, or to bring in staff on short term contracts, or to recruit more full-time staff. The last option will be taken if it fits in with long term staff planning. Difficulties with resource level occur not only with development staff: data preparation may create an overload which has to be accommodated by using an external bureau. There is also the possibility of user staff being overloaded at any phase, particularly during implementation. Their commitment to the project is crucial and must be secured. It may therefore be expedient to obtain temporary clerical staff to replace users who will then be allowed to concentrate their efforts within the project. User management commitment is equally crucial – the possibility of other managers in the organization giving assistance with normal work should be explored.

Assessment of in-house computing resources

The construction phase of the project may require levels of computing resource which exceed or differ from those required for live running or for any other planned development work. Action is needed to get access to these special development facilities on a short term basis.

Equipment can be rented, leased lines installed for access to remote computer services, or the development team temporarily moved to a special site where appropriate facilities exist. In this kind of situation where the development facility and the live facility differ so markedly, an extra area of uncertainty is introduced. Careful checking of the

transfer from one environment to the other will therefore need to be planned.

Using external staff

In assessing the resource problems associated with a project, the opportunity for using staff from consultants, software houses and specialist contracting agencies will arise. This solves the immediate problem of workload but introduces several others.

Negotiation

A dependable agency must be identified. Reputation is everything, because no worthwhile guarantees of performance can be obtained from any agency. The precise nature of charging, the period and continuity of commitment, the selection of staff to be contracted and their management must all be discussed.

Commitment

Contract staff may have the required skills but lack the enthusiasm for the project that in-house staff have.

Missed learning opportunities

Experience of the development work, including use of any new software or hardware products, will be carried away with the contract staff and lost to the organization.

Further support difficulties

Even if the documentation for system maintenance is first rate, future support will be rendered more difficult through not having easy access to the relevant development staff, particularly in the early days of live running.

Sub-contracting

Major portions of the project may be sub-contracted to a software consultancy house if serious in-house skill or resource deficiencies exist. All the points concerning the use of external staff apply in this instance but are more strongly emphasized. An additional problem is that of review and management. The in-house project manager will be placed in the same position as a user manager, able to view the project by way of a series of widely spaced snapshots but not able to assess situations as they arise and act quickly and perhaps informally to keep the project on course.

The negotiation of sub-contracted work is crucial. The in-house project manager should ensure certain key areas are considered:

What design and specification methods will be used?

What standards of documentation will be observed?

What precisely is to be handed over?

What performance is required? (run times, on-line response times, main and magnetic store occupancy)

What is the timescale for delivery? (Staged or otherwise)

What is the method of calculating charges?

What is the method of payment and when is this required?

What acceptance trials will there be, when will they be held and how will they be related to payment?

What methods of progress review will be used and what will be available for examination?

What will be the routine for amendments, including charges?

What will be the rights of cancellation or delay?

A full-scale contract must be constructed and expert advice should be sought. However, a firm contract is no compensation for the failure to deliver a system, and subcontracting agencies should be carefully selected on the basis of their reputation and relevant experience if major disasters are to be avoided.

Phase breakdown and estimation

Defining tasks

Immediately prior to any phase of a project, but more particularly prior to the analysis, design and construction phases, a detailed breakdown of the intended activity into tasks should be performed. This will override the global estimating which has so far sufficed for the phase. This task analysis is now standard practice and is motivated by three prime benefits.

1 The discipline helps to identify the complex detail of what is needed and thus gives greater accuracy in estimating delivery.
2 Chopping the work into distinct tasks allows it to be distributed among a team of people and provides them with targets.
3 The definition of tasks, each with its own deadline, permits effective management of the phase as a whole.

Choosing tasks

There has to be considerable flexibility in defining tasks, but some features are intrinsic to the task

principle. First, the work content of the task should be within certain limits. The ideal task is 3-5 working days, but the variation allowed may be as wide as 1-20 days. The lower limit is defined by seeking a meaningful unit of responsibility for the individual and by recognizing the problem of attempting to monitor too many small tasks. The upper limit is set so that a manager can obtain access to the outputs of the completed task before too much effort is wasted. If a small number of large tasks is defined then statements on project progress cannot confidently be made.

Secondly, the task must be conceived in such a way that its completion is a well-defined 'success unit'. It is this latter principle that causes the variation in task size. A few illustrative examples of success units, taken from the phases in which they occur, are shown in Table 4.3. A task constitutes a success unit if the end product of the task is some item (document, program, chart or agreement) the existence and quality of which can be assessed. This idea leads to distinctive structuring within the phase. The idea of a program may have to be broken down into several tasks or success units: design of the structure, coding, preparation of the test plan, preparation of the test data, production of a clean listing, successful execution of the various test paths, and final documentation. Each of these tasks can be assessed for work content and, just as importantly, the achievement of the task is also assessable.

Table 4.3 Phases and success units

Phase	Success unit
Feasibility	Conduct, record and check out an interview.
	Draw up DCF analysis for alternative solutions.
	Prepare presentation to directors.
Analysis	Construct, review and finalize overall DFD.
	Complete second stage data model.
	Record all critical document turnaround times.
Design	Specify all screen layouts.
	Specify interactive validation requirements.
	Prepare system testing plan.
Construction	Prepare program structure.
	Produce test plan and test data.
	Conduct month-end test.

Estimating work content
In the detailed estimation of the work content of a task, the abilities of the person who is to complete that task are important. In medium and long range planning actions it has to be accepted that some sort of standard time is used, but when planning for the immediate phase we can be more accurate.

Where do the estimates come from? Past project history guides us, and a look at the records is instructive and often salutary. However, when working at a detailed level the most accepted approach is that of discussion and negotiation between the project manager and the person to whom the task is to be assigned. If the latter lacks experience then tasks will be kept particularly short to allow frequent supervisory intervention and to counteract a well-known tendency for optimism and over-commitment which afflicts most junior programmers and analysts. The more junior the worker then the greater will be the input by the project manager, who will use his experience, his assessment of the individual's potential and his records of estimating similar tasks in the past. With more senior personnel the project manager will allow them a bigger say in estimating the task's work content. Under no circumstances is it wise for the project manager to attempt to squeeze unrealistically tight estimates from an individual, or to set up dummy figures as an unreachable target. Such approaches to management have no place in an environment where frank, accurate communication is vital.

The negotiation of a task estimate is concluded by the completion of a task sheet which may be filed or issued depending on the needs of the moment. An example is shown in Figure 4.3. Provision is made on the task sheet for recording the time spent and any events that occurred within the task. This will encourage the use of completed task sheets for reference purposes in future project estimating.

Mapping work content into elapsed time
There are many reasons why the elapsed time for a task will be longer than its work content; examples of one group of reasons are listed below:

People required for interview are unavailable.
Documentation typing is held up.
Access to the computer involves delays.
A key manual is being used elsewhere.
A manufacturer's specification proves ambiguous and a query is raised.

In such cases the *key* resource, i.e. the person assigned to the task, is still available but other

TASK SHEET

PROJECT: *3147*   PHASE: *SD*   TASK: *14*

DESCRIPTION:

> *Prepare a schedule of validation requirements for the on-line transaction set. Check-out design with users.*

PRE-REQUISITE TASKS: *6, 10, 13.*   DAYS' EFFORT

ACTIVITIES

Activity	Days
Discuss details with section manager and at least two clerical staff.	*1½*
Draw up schedule of validation using FORMS-2.	*2*
Demonstrate and adjust the validations.	*1½*
Input details to Data Dictionary.	*1*

ESTIMATE OF TOTAL EFFORT REQUIRED	*6*

TASK ASSIGNED TO: *JRB*

ACTUAL START DATE: *03/02/87*

ACTUAL FINISH DATE: *13/02/87*

ACTUAL DAYS BOOKED TO THIS TASK: *7½*

COMMENT:

> *One clerk had been absent from the demonstration and subsequently raised some issues that required corrections to be input to the Data Dictionary.*

Figure 4.3   *Example task sheet*

resources on which that person depends are not. It is therefore possible, and very likely, that a second assigned task will be picked up and progressed until either another impasse is reached or the original task is released from its dependency. There is a limit as to how many tasks an individual can cope with, and perhaps three or four is a sensible limit. Beyond this the time spent familiarizing oneself with each task would become excessive. Another group of reasons for delay is concerned with the person to whom the task is assigned:

A planned holiday is taken.
A planned training course is taken.
Urgent maintenance of an existing system is required.
Sickness intervenes.
Review and planning meetings are attended.

Allowing for this sort of interruption is essential if the overall phase planning is to be sensible. The planned holidays and courses can be allowed for accurately as known blocks of time.

Other unplanned time loss can only be allowed for on a global basis. Past records for the department will be a guide, and it would not be uncommon to allow for one day out of five to cater for these less predictable items. This extra time should probably not be added into the task estimates pro-rata, but should be allowed for in the scheduling and timetabling activities discussed in the next section.

Phase contingency and budget
After all this careful estimating there remains the possibility of the planning being disrupted by some unforeseen event. An indication of the likelihood of this is incorporated in the nature of the project itself. The project manager will address himself to five key questions.

1 Is there a strong commitment to the agreed objectives of the project by the users?
2 Are the user departments experienced in implementing computer systems of this type?
3 Have the development staff appropriate experience and skills for this project?
4 Is the software environment a settled one with no major new products?
5 Is the hardware environment a settled one with no extensive enhancements expected?

Each answer to these five questions can be marked as in Table 4.4.

For each mark totalled out of the five questions allow 2%, to give a total in the range of 10%–50%, representing the amount of contingency time which should be allowed. Scores over 30% indicate projects which are likely to produce many unforeseen difficulties and are high risk.

Having settled on a contingency element the planner and project manager will introduce it into the phase and monitor its consumption carefully.

The budget
Estimation of work content and elapsed time planning are essential if the phase is to be successfully managed. But before the phase begins there may be a requirement to review the project's viability. The most likely point in a project when this could occur is after design and specification but before any construction has begun. Those sponsoring the project (e.g. the steering committee) seek the opportunity to review the costs and benefits before committing themselves further. Thus the sponsors will want to know the cost of the phase. The preparation of the budget to answer this question will depend on the relationship of system development to the organization as a whole. If the relationship is one where development costs are charged out, then there are agreed rates for the work. In this case

Table 4.4 Contingency scores

Answer	Yes	Yes with some minor reservations	Significant doubts in some areas	Major reservations in key areas	Emphatically no!
Mark	1	2	3	4	5

these rates will already incorporate the overheads of systems development. The budget is then prepared on the basis of the total of the estimated task work content together with the phase contingency. This detail is worked out in the form of a monthly spending forecast inclusive of projected charges for machine usage and expenses incurred. These costs then represent forecasts of the bills which the sponsor will have to pay to obtain delivery of the system. By contrasting

these with the proposed benefits an up-to-date view of the project's viability can be obtained.

If a charge out system is not used, then the total elapsed time of the phase will be of more interest. In this case, where the cost of running systems development is simply carried as an overhead to the organization, the important issue is for senior management to arrange properly the priorities to ensure that key systems are brought in on-time.

Project networks

Breaking down the phases into tasks provides many benefits but introduces a few problems. The divide and rule approach to project planning implicit in task definition gives the 'ruler' the responsibility of ensuring that the divided parts actually fit together at the right time. One aid to this synchronization is the construction of a project network. The network is particularly valuable for relating the obvious system development tasks (interviews, data design, tests) to less obvious but crucial project activities such as obtaining delivery of hardware items and negotiating agreements. The creation and maintenance of project networks can be achieved using various software packages available for micro, mini or mainframe computers. The calculation and analysis performed later in this section could be undertaken by a computer-based package. For very large projects with hundreds of linked activities the benefits to the project manager are obvious.

Constructing a network

Each task identified within a phase is entered on to the network. The important details which need to be known are the *duration* of the task and the identity of those other tasks which must be complete before it can commence. The task can be drawn as an *activity* and an *event*.

The event should be thought of as the measurable or observable culmination of the activity. Our care in defining tasks as clearly

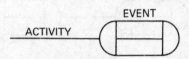

defined success units will help when constructing a meaningful network.

The strict interpretation of dependencies between activities may lead to further careful consideration of task content. Consider the two fragments of network in Figure 4.4 (page 84).

The activity occurring between events 1 and 2 in (a) has been explored further in (b) to reveal the true dependency: design of the interface programs can take place as soon as the package is identified and need not wait for its delivery.

Figure 4.5 (page 85) uses activities on arrows to define a network of dependent tasks for a phase plan. One problem associated with using networks is shown by the use of the dummy activity between events 7 and 8. Activity I can be commenced as soon as activity D is complete. It is estimated to take no more than fifteen days but cannot be marked complete until activity H is known to be finished. Thus a dummy activity of zero duration starting after event 7 and preceding event 8 is inserted to establish the required precedence. The dummy activity consumes no manpower resources but is used in the various calculations shown below and can play a significant part in identifying a network's critical

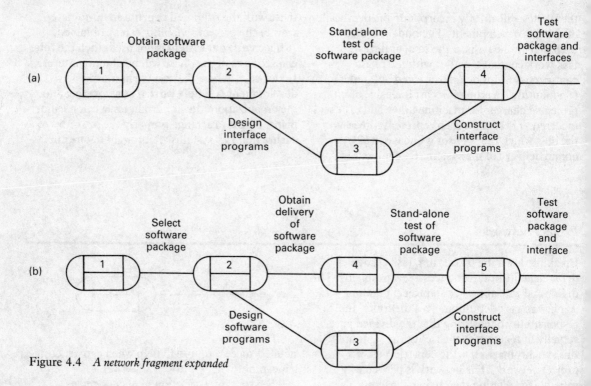

Figure 4.4   *A network fragment expanded*

path. Earliest and latest times for each event can be calculated and are shown on the example in Figure 4.5. The *earliest* time for an event (e.g. event 11) is calculated by adding the duration (15) of the preceding activity (N) to the earliest time of the preceding event (event 9, earliest time 113). The result (128) is the earliest time at which event 11 can occur. Where several preceding activities lead to an event then the largest value is taken for the earliest time.

The *latest* time for an event (e.g. event 6) is calculated by subtracting the duration (90) of the succeeding activity (L) from the latest time of the succeeding event (event 9, latest time 130). The result (40) is the latest time at which event 6 can occur. Where several activities succeed an event (e.g. event 5) then the smallest value is taken for the latest finish time.

The *event slack* can now be calculated for each event as the difference between its earliest and latest times.

Table 4.5 (page 86) shows how these event times can be used to calculate an important value

known as the *float* of an activity. It is the difference betweeen the activity's estimated duration and the total elapsed time (known as the *activity span*) during which the activity could be started and completed without affecting the total project duration. Activities which have a positive float thus have a built-in buffer against their duration estimates being too low. Activities without such a float are critical because any slippage in their completion inevitably causes lateness in the project as a whole. Such activities when linked together define the *critical path* of the network. Project managers will wish to monitor such activities carefully. However, even before the phase commences, the act of creating the network has already proved beneficial by drawing attention to certain crucial activities whose estimates can now be double-checked before being confirmed.

It is worth noting that the dummy activity created to establish the precedence between events 7 and 8 in Figure 4.5 plays a crucial role in the identification of the critical path in this network

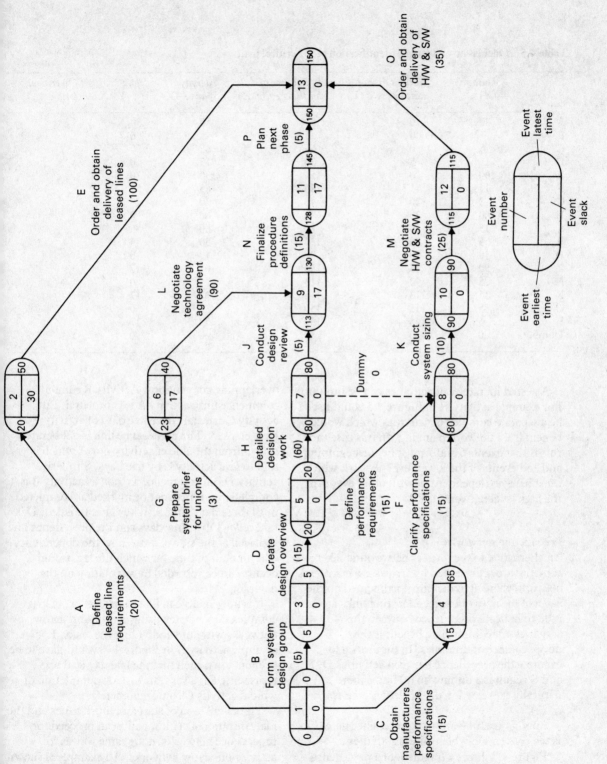

Figure 4.5 *Network of the design and procurement phase of a system development project*

Table 4.5   Calculation of float and identification of the critical path

Activity	Duration (X)	Earliest time of starting event (Y)	Latest time of finishing event (Z)	Activity span (Z–Y)	Float ((Z–Y)–X)	On critical path ?
A	20	0	50	50	30	
B	5	0	5	5	0	√
C	15	0	65	65	50	
D	15	5	20	15	0	√
E	100	20	150	130	30	
F	15	15	80	65	50	
G	3	20	40	20	17	
H	60	20	80	60	0	√
I	15	20	80	60	45	
J	5	80	130	50	45	
K	10	80	90	10	0	√
L	90	23	130	107	17	
M	25	90	115	25	0	√
N	15	113	145	32	17	
O	35	115	150	35	0	√
P	5	128	150	22	17	
Dummy	0	80	80	0	0	√

A nested hierarchy of activities can be built up. For example activity H in Figure 4.5 could itself be a separate complex of activities which would benefit from network planning. In this case the rule is that events 5 and 7 must be the beginning and end events of the lower level network which must have no dependencies with other events in the high level network.

Precedence networks

An alternative to the form of networking where activities are represented by arrows is a *precedence* network where activities are documented on the *nodes* of the network and connecting links are used to indicate precedence between the activities. One immediate benefit is the disappearance of dummies. In Figure 4.6 for example the precedence between activities D, E and G requires a dummy in (a) but is more naturally expressed in the precedence network in (b).

Another useful feature of precedence networks is the convention which allows activities to overlap.

Figure 4.7 shows a fragment of a precedence network illustrating two aspects of the overlapping conventions. Activity B cannot commence until activity A is completed. But activity C can start once five days of activity A have elapsed. The precedence line is deliberately drawn from the side of activity box A which is said to *lead* activity C by five days. Similarly activity D can commence as soon as activity B is complete but it may not be marked as completed until three days after activity C has finished. D is said to *lag* C by three days and the precedence line is placed at the side of D to show the dependency. The amount of time for which the lag or lead occurs can be recorded by annotating on the diagram.

It is not possible to illustrate this sort of complex dependency using activity-on-arrow networks without subdividing the tasks. For example activity A in Figure 4.7 would have to be broken down such that the five day lead was represented as a separate task on completion of which, activity C could commence.

The calculation of start and finish times and the identification of critical paths can proceed for precedence networks in the same way as for activity-on-arrow networks. An example is shown in Figure 4.8 (page 88).

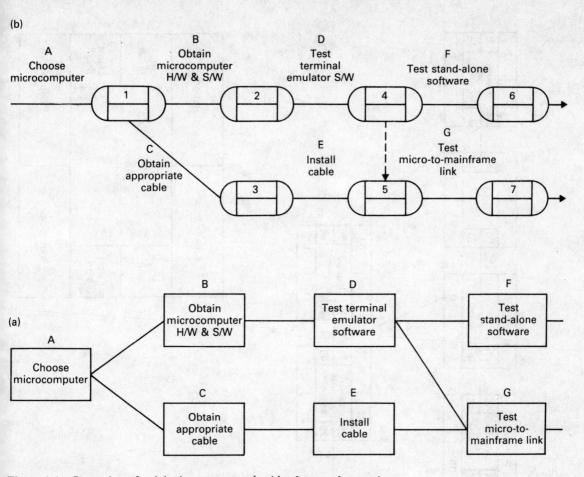

Figure 4.6 *Comparison of activity-in-arrow network with a framework network*

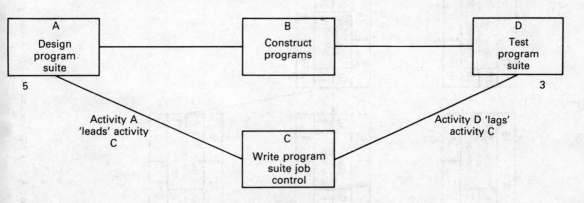

Figure 4.7 *Illustration of leads and lags in a precedence network*

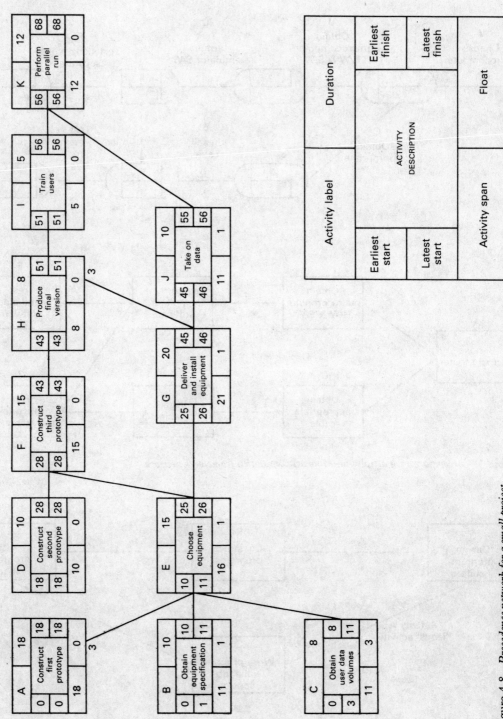

Figure 4.8   *Precedence network for a small project*

Exercises

1 When reviewing the success of planning for systems development it is often found that analysis and design phases are performed close to plan whilst construction and implementation are the main cause of overrunning. Why do you think this is so?

2 A pool of 24 analyst/programmers is assigned to a development project and it is required to split them into teams. Assume equal team sizes and assume that each team member communicates only with members of his or her own team apart from the team leader who also communicates with all the other team leaders. What team size gives a minimum of lines of communication in the total pool?

3 As well as engaging a computer consultancy to undertake one selected project, it is possible to subcontract to them the whole of a computer services operation, this is usually called facilities management.

   Identify, for a financial director, the positive benefits of taking this approach and suggest circumstances when it may be particularly appropriate to do this.

4 The following tasks have turned out to be too big with respect to an installation standard (i.e. they are estimated to require more than ten days effort). Show how they can be redefined such that the new tasks retain identity and the ability to be realistically assessed for completion.

   Evaluate a new software product for screen formatting – 15 days. Train six stock recording clerks to use a new on-line stock records system – 12 days.

5 In Figure 4.8 activity H can lag activity G by three days. On reconsidering the network this is thought optimistic, and it is now thought that activity G should be completed before activity H is commenced. Assuming that the other values remain the same, redraw the network and identify the changes which will interest the project manager.

Further reading

Brooks, F., *The Mythical Man Month*, Addison Wesley 1982.

Johnson, J. R., *A working measure of productivity*, in *Managing for Data Processing Productivity*, QED 1980.

Lockyer, K., *Critical Path Analysis*, Pitman 1984

NCC, *Guidelines for Computer Managers*, NCC, 1981.

5 Project monitoring

Introduction

Project planning is the process of matching the objectives which have been devised for a project to the resources available, and producing plans. Project monitoring is the activity which observes and assesses the extent to which actual progress matches these plans. Project monitoring is therefore, very much concerned with the detail of the phases, tasks and networks produced in the planning process. More fundamentally the objective of monitoring is to identify whether or not the system being developed will in some way fail to match expectations. Four sources of danger exist for system development projects once they are launched.

The **system components** produced may vary unacceptably from what is required. The variance could be in terms of response times, job run time, accuracy, appearance, resilience or many other features.

The **cost** of the system development project may be significantly higher or lower than expected. In the former case there exists the possibility that the cost/benefit balance may move from acceptable to unacceptable.

The **time** scheduled for the project may be consumed rapidly without a corresponding completion of tasks. This results in delivery dates being missed. Possibly these dates are crucially related to important check-points such as the end of the tax year or start of a new contract.

The **commitment** of those involved in the project may begin to flag. Changes in management, organization structure or the announcement of new products can create such situations.

Monitoring must be capable of identifying difficulties in these areas. The identification should take place early so that the full

Table 5.1 Types of reviewing methods

Level	Type of review	Frequency	Characteristics of review
1	Phase review	At end of each phase	Report circulated, presented and discussed
			Major feasibility issues reviewed
			Overall costs and time-scale for next phase included
2	Progress review	Variable between 1–4 times per month dependent on age of project	Progress summaries circulated
			Resource assignments made
			Key dates fixed
			Motivation and inter-group pressure problems debated
3	Design reviews and walkthroughs	On demand and thus approximately one per week as system components become assessable	Centred on quality of the chosen system component e.g. data design, program structure
4	Personal progress monitoring	Varies dependent on experience of person, daily for juniors, weekly for seniors	Concentrates on tasks in hand
			Discussion on difficulties, tactics and actual achievement

implications of the trend can be assessed and remedial action considered. The range of dangers is wide, and monitoring techniques are similarly diverse. We are looking for both small and large problems, so a hierarchy of reviewing methods is needed, each with different cycles, methods and audiences. This is shown in Table 5.1. The foundation for this monitoring is at level 4, where the project manager is in contact with those completing the various tasks identified within the project. Here it is possible for the project manager to obtain a view of all aspects of the project, including the quality of an individual's effort, the motivation and commitment of those involved, any impending system performance problems or the start of an outward drift on completion dates. Formal monitoring records will add useful detail to this impressionistic view of the project. However, a project manager will attempt always to obtain both formal and informal views and must therefore ensure that opportunities to be involved in the project are taken up and excessive reliance on written records does not occur.

Collection of monitoring data

The smallest unit in a project is the task. Accurate monitoring therefore requires precise records of task progress. The basic unit used to achieve this is the *weekly timesheet* (Figure 5.1). Here individuals record how their time has been spent. Because for a development worker most activity will be in pursuit of project tasks it is convenient to assign project and task codes to all likely activities: training, leave, union meetings etc. This extra detail is useful in providing a basis for future global estimating and charge-out rate decisions by giving figures for productive time as a percentage of total time booked. Timesheet details enable the actual hours expended on tasks to be compared with the forecasted time. The purpose of the *Time to complete* column is to improve the accuracy of a review by including estimates for any tasks uncompleted at the time the review takes place. Because the project manager will be maintaining contact with most members of the project team these estimates will come from agreements reached between the manager and the individual completing the timesheet.

The true value of the data collected in timesheets is realized when producing management review material. A monitoring format found useful by most managers particularly during the design and construction phases of a project is the annotated Gantt Chart (Figure 5.2, page 94). This is drawn up on the basis of the tasks defined and the people to whom they are allocated. Leave, training courses and other known non-project activities are shown on the charts. Tasks progress can be recorded by shading along the bar to represent the state of completion of the task. At a defined review date it is possible to identify all the tasks which are behind and those which are on time or ahead. This chart forms the basis of manpower management and can prompt the redistribution of tasks between individuals to ensure that the project progresses efficiently.

In the execution of this low level monitoring the importance of careful task definition can be appreciated. Tasks will ideally have been defined as being 1-20 days in size, and their completion clearly identified by the production of physical output. There can then be some confidence in progress summaries based on the task monitoring principle. Poor task definition leads to a variety of problems. If tasks are too long then at any one review there will be several unfinished tasks each of which may have a large unexpended man-day content. This leads to uncertainties about how much has been truly achieved. The same effect is produced where tasks have no clear endpoint with a physical output (e.g. a design document, manual, or program listing). Such tasks are difficult to pin down as being finished. Without hard evidence to permit precise monitoring, there may be a tendency to tick off a poorly defined task which in fact is not properly complete and continues to absorb effort for weeks to come.

Projects will also consume a variety of other resources, like computer usage,

PIZZERIA MARCELLO

4 Albion Place,
Sunderland.
Telephone: Wearside 5671032.

V.A.T. Reg. No. 495 9636 76

```
        23-11-88
           20:37                    14787
        TABLE NO.                        4
             2X                    @1.05
        ZUPPA/POMODO               -2.10
        POLLO IMPERI               -6.35
        BISTECCA PIZ               -6.90
        ASTI MARTINI               -7.40
             5No
   10 NB                      -22.75
             2X                    @1.10
        CAPPUCINO                  -2.20
        BANANA SPLIT               -1.65
             3No
   05 NB                      -26.60
             0No
        CH                    -26.60
```

TABLE 4

WAITER M

COVERS 2

Sicilian Pasta Co. Ltd.

TIME SHEET

NAME: T. BOOTH STAFF CODE: 1 0 3 4 GRADE: S/2 WK END DATE (DD MM YY): 13 03 88

Name and task description	Code	Phase code	Task number	Mon HRS	Tue HRS	Wed HRS	Thu HRS	Fri HRS	Sat HRS	Sun HRS	TOTAL HRS	TIME TO COMPLETE DAYS D•D
Axle divn. nominal ledger review	A D 7	S D	0 0 0 1	0 1							0 0 1	•
Axle divn. nominal ledger format	A D 7	S D	0 0 1 2	0 6	0 7		0 5	0 5			0 2 3	1 • 5
												•
Press divn. stock recording maintenance	P D 8	M 7	1 0 3 4			0 8	0 2				0 1 0	•
Training: SAA seminar	T R 1	9 9	2 0 0 1					0 2			0 0 2	•
												•
												•
												•
												•
												•
TOTALS				0 7	0 7	0 8	0 7	0 7			0 3 6	

Approved

Overtime authorized

Figure 5.1 *Example timesheet*

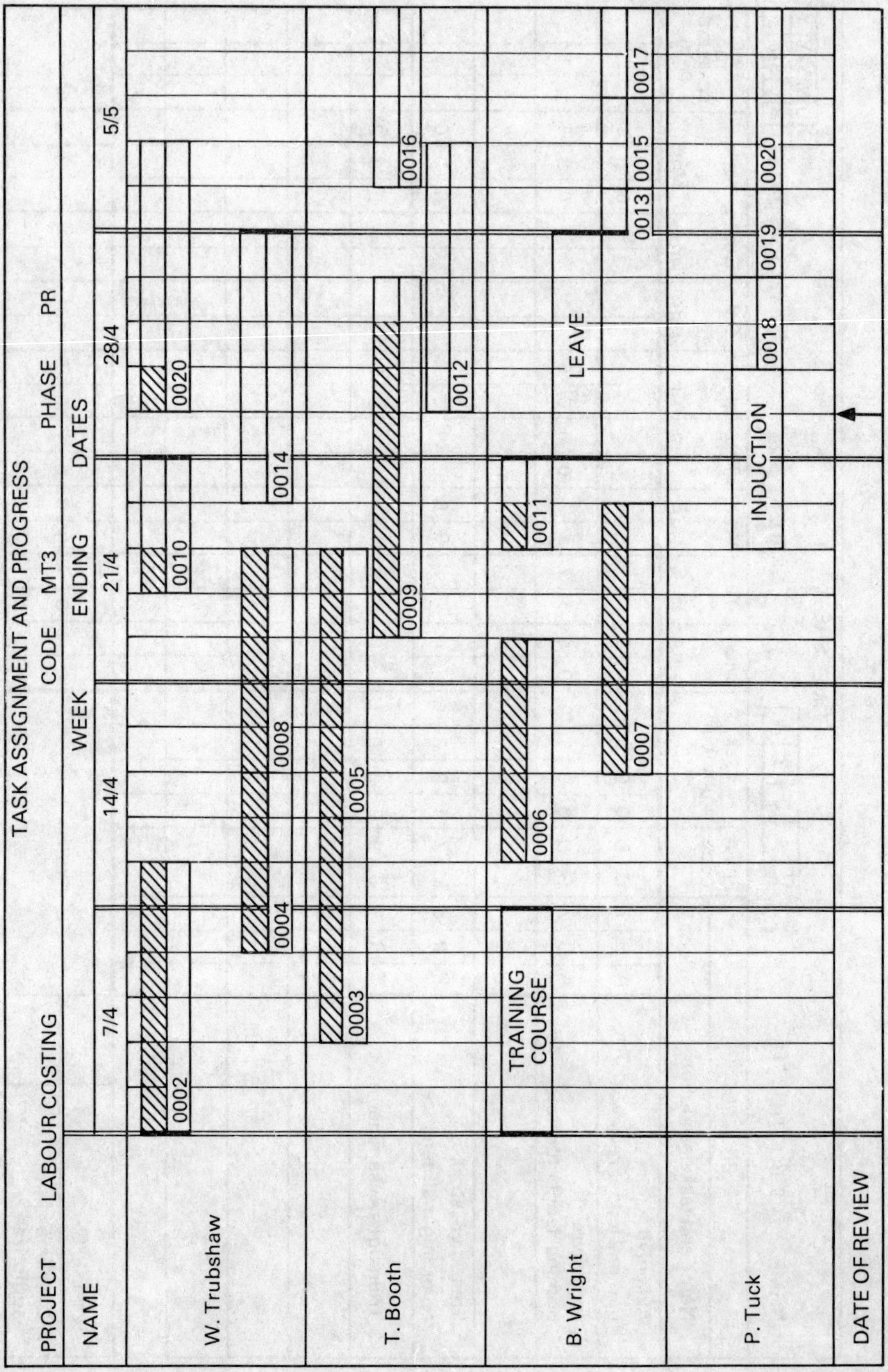

Figure 5.2   *Annotated Gantt chart*

telecommunications, travel and accommodation expenses, consultants, typing, printing, copying and distribution. Various other categories could be relevant depending on the terms of reference of the project. These items will be collected into any statement concerning the overall financial position of the project. It is possible, and in many cases desirable, to identify this expenditure at the task level. This may be particularly useful in relating consumption of computer time to a particular programming task. In other cases this sort of expenditure will be simply attributable to the whole phase and reported at that level.

Collecting these miscellaneous costs can often be achieved as a by-product of other systems. Accommodation and travel expenses usually have to receive management approval, providing the opportunity for these items to be coded and noted. Computer usage can probably be monitored as part of a general system being run by the operations department for the recovery of costs from those who use their services for live systems.

Presentation of monitoring data

Costs

Reviewing bodies will be interested in current and projected costs for the project. Phase, not task, level breakdowns are good enough for most reviews. Table 5.2 (page 96) shows an example of how such a statement might appear. Only the current phase is shown in detailed form. Cost variances arising over the most recent period are clearly identified and will be discussed in some detail. Two sensible responses to variances are possible. Either some management action is agreed which it is hoped will eliminate the variances by reducing the estimates to complete, or the variances will be authorized and will appear accumulated into column (b) at the next review.

In addition to forecasts of cost totals and variances, the project cash flow forecast will be of interest and Figure 5.3 (page 96) shows an example of how a bar chart can be used to illustrate this.

Timescales

Is the project on time and will implementation be completed by the original estimated date? Even if costs are being successfully controlled there may be key dates which cannot be missed. Data presented for review must therefore show how well tasks are running to schedule. The annotated Gantt chart (Figure 5.2) is useful for this purpose. Another approach is shown in Figure 5.4 (page 97) where a network is drawn against a time grid

and progress is indicated by shading out events which have occurred. At the review date it is possible to see whether or not events to the left of the review time are all recorded (as they should be). An event which is late must have one or more overrunning activities leading up to it and these can be discussed with a view to absorbing the problem. The full effect of late running activities can be calculated by re-assessing all the later completion dates in the network. The effect of the delay on the project as a whole may be containable if none of the late activities is on the critical path. However, the network should be completely reassessed, taking into consideration any revised durations. It is possible that a new critical path may emerge and this would result in new monitoring priorities.

Efficiency indicators

As well as the pictorial impression gained from looking at Gantt charts and networks it is useful to prepare quantitative indicators of the performance of a project. Sometimes overspending or late running can be acceptable if other aspects of the project are seen to be under control. It is desirable therefore, to formulate and monitor indicators to show how successful the project is in deploying the required manpower efficiently. At a given point during the life of a project, we make the following measurements:

Table 5.2 Project cost summary

Project Financial consolidation **Code** FD04   **Review period** Monthly **Ending** 15/4

Phase / Expense category	Original estimate (a)	Agreed amendments (b)	Revised estimate (c=a+b)	Spent this period (d)	Spent in prior periods (e)	Spent to date (f=d+e)	Estimate to complete (g)	Current phase estimate (h=f+g)	Projected variance (i=c−h)
FEASIBILITY									
Total	7700	1500	9200	—	10500	10500	—	10500	(1300)
ANALYSIS AND DESIGN									
Total	18750	3000	21750	—	20500	20500	—	20500	1250
CONSTRUCTION (CURRENT)									
Manpower	33000	4000	37000	5600	21200	26800	14600	41400	(4400)
Computer	15000	—	15000	2200	5000	7200	6500	13700	1300
Expense	7500	500	8000	1300	3800	5100	3500	8600	(600)
Total	55500	4500	60000	9100	30000	39100	24600	63700	(3700)
IMPLEMENTATION									
Total	9500	—	9500	—	—	—	9500	9500	—
Grand total	91450	9000	100450	9100	61000	70100	34100	104200	(3750)

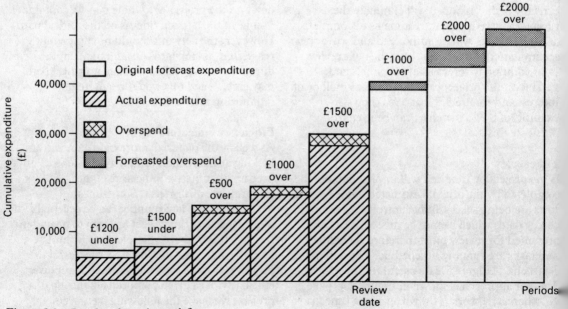

Figure 5.3 *Bar chart for project cash flow*

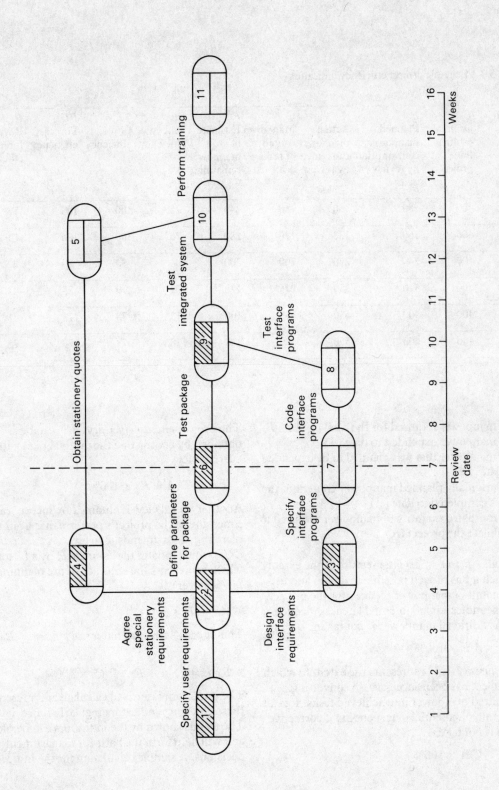

Figure 5.4 *Network used to illustrate project progress*

Table 5.3   Example project efficiency indicators

Month of review	T Original estimate for project	P Planned manpower consumption by review date	A Actual manpower consumed by review date	C Manpower content of tasks achieved	R Estimate of manpower remaining	SE Schedule efficiency	CE Cost efficiency	FE Forecast efficiency	RFE Revised forecasted efficiency
Jan	400	80	60	60	340	75	100	100	78
Feb	400	160	120	120	280	75	100	100	81
Mar	400	240	250	200	200	104	80	89	82
Apr	400	320	350	275	120	109	79	85	82
May	400	400	450	350	100	112	78	73	71
June	400	400	550	400	0	138	73	73	72

the manpower required for the total project (T)
the manpower expended to date (A)
the manpower that was planned to be expended to date (P)
the originally planned manpower content of the tasks completed to date (C)
the estimated quantity of manpower required to complete the project (R)

Schedule efficiency (SE) is a measure of the extent to which it has proved possible to obtain and use the amount of manpower pledged for the project. It is one indication of potential lateness if action to obtain additional manpower is not taken.

$$SE = A/P \times 100\%$$

Cost efficiency (CE) represents the extent to which the project has been successful in converting committed manpower into achieved tasks. It is an indication of potential overspending if corrective action is not taken.

$$CE = C/A \times 100\%$$

The project *forecast efficiency* (FE) can be obtained by contrasting the original plan with the current view

$$FE = T/(A + R) \times 100\%$$

Another useful view is obtained by incorporating a measure of the project's performance against its planning. This amends R to give a *revised estimate* (RE) which inflates the estimate R by a factor which represents the accuracy of the planning so far (see over)

$$RE = R \times P/C$$

This suggests a *revised forecasted efficiency* (RFE) as

$$RFE = T/(A + R \times P/C) \times 100\%$$

The important issue is to calculate and present these efficiency indicators regularly for review. The trends shown by the indicators can be plotted and will help form the basis for management decisions. A sample calculation for the indicators

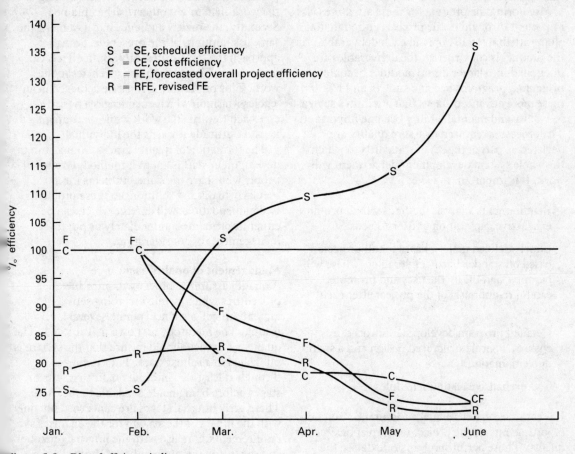

Figure 5.5   *Plot of efficiency indicators*

...s shown in Table 5.3. A plot of the indicators is ...hown in Figure 5.5.

The plot illustrates the early difficulty in ...obilizing sufficient manpower to support the ...roject plan. At this stage the cost and forecast efficiency indicators show nothing untoward but the revised forecast efficiency indicator reflects the divergence from planning. As manpower is brought into the project the indicators reflect the efficiency of its use.

Monitoring for quality

...n monitoring for quality the project manager ...ssesses both the general and the specific ...ttributes of that group of deliverables which go to make up the software product and its associated documentation. The general attributes of interest are completeness, correctness, reliability and maintainability. Specifically, he will want to test that each deliverable meets the functional and performance criteria of the user and any affected third parties.

Monitoring the product for these attributes is important throughout the project, although not all the attributes will apply to each deliverable. As the product is constructed, the deliverables are integrated into larger units (modules become programs, programs become suites), and it is at these more advanced stages that attributes such as reliability and maintainability become important. The processes required to assure quality are declared as part of the set of standards to which the whole system development department will work. It is important to have:

Requirements analysis methods which promote exhaustive exploration of users' needs.

Clearly defined major phases for all projects, based on standardized deliverables. These will permit a sign-off by the user and promote careful re-appraisal of the project after each phase.

Detailed program development procedures to ensure a logical, structured design and a sound implementation.

Comprehensive testing schedules.

It is common to have a quality assurance function, reporting outside the project team, responsible for quality. Those performing this role devise the processes, sell them to the respective project managers and their teams, and monitor their success.

Self-regulating quality assurance

One approach is for the quality assurance officer to promote an internal concern for quality. Team members are encouraged to view high quality production as part of their professionalism and invited to work together to produce quality items. This leads to the adoption of internal review mechanisms.

One example is the walkthrough. A team member conducts a technical presentation of his work (e.g. a database design). The audience is 'walked through' the work step by step. This has two effects. First the discipline of preparing a presentation leads to a deeper understanding of the work than might otherwise be obtained. Secondly, the review audience may not make the same assumptions as the presenter, or may approach the topic differently. Both effects can flush out problems and inconsistencies in the work. This public airing must be achieved in an 'egoless' fashion which encourages a positive approach towards the work while discouraging a negative attitude towards the individual.

The formation of quality circles among system development staff is another method. Groups of people who share the same problems meet regularly to discuss solutions to those problems. Recommendations will emerge which can be either implemented immediately or put to management for consideration.

Management of quality assurance

A quality assurance officer will introduce procedures which, while including self-regulation, will also incorporate several levels of testing. The hierarchy is shown in Table 5.4. The quality assurance should ensure that the system is published in a robust state. Thus it may go through at least two internal quality assurance stages before being made available to the users. These early internal stages are concerned not only with the fitness of the system for the end user's requirements, but also with the internal operation and the future maintainability of the system.

User validation is a carefully controlled live usage of the system. There will be extensive support for the users during this stage. There will be several system 'releases', which incorporate amendments to faults unearthed by users, in the first few weeks. The incidence of faults, the frequency of system releases and the consequent level of support should gradually diminish.

A further stage may be necessary for software which is to be marketed. Such software products may undergo certification by an independent auditing body which will certify the extent to which the product matches its specification and documentation.

Table 5.4 Hierarchy of system quality assurance

Level of quality assurance and who actions it	Objectives of the quality assurance procedure	Methods used in the procedure
System testing The development team	To establish conformity of the system to the specifications. Many of these specifications are internally generated for low-level items	Module tests JCL-linked tests Suite tests Performance tests Recovery tests
Verification The quality assurance function	To establish that the system conforms to: users' functional requirements, users' performance requirements and standards for operation and maintenance	Simulated live environment using 'borrowed' data, terminals, clerical staff etc. as required. Daily, weekly, monthly cycles are explored
Validation User staff	To use the system in a live environment in order that operational dificulties can be resolved and acceptance of the system by the user agreed	The system is made fully operational in the knowledge that some failures will occur. The system goes through several releases to overcome these
* Certification Independent audit body	To establish that the software product is adequately and accurately described by its marketing methods and documentation	Working from system documentation, tests are devised and applied which will endorse the product's claims

*Relevant to marketed software products only

Review findings

Reviews take place daily, weekly, monthly and at major phase milestones. A review will occasionally find that everything is going according to plan. More frequently the review will consider difficulties which beset the projects, and will agree appropriate action. Some examples of problems and their sources are shown in Table 5.5 (page 102).

Responding to these problems so as to improve the situation for the current project requires careful concentration. It is easy to get distracted into strategic issues. For example, if projects are frequently affected by organization structure changes then projects should be shorter and less ambitious. Similarly, if supplier problems continually occur then supply policy should be examined. However, although the project reviews will be encouraged to provide feedback of this type to the policy-makers they must tackle the immediate problem with tactical actions.

Tactical actions will be examined under the three headings used in Table 5.5.

Environmental problems

Significant problems of this sort must be absorbed into the project and will result in replanning after a reassessment of objectives, requirements, design etc. Recosting and feasibility assessment will be needed. One of the chief dangers is to project staff morale, because useful work may have to be shelved. The replanned project can then be launched with some explanatory meetings for the team and subsequently reviewed and controlled as normal.

Table 5.5 Project problems and their sources

Problems with the system environment	Problems with system development staff	Problems with system development tools
Unexpected statutory changes by government	Staff turnover exceeds expectations	Delays in the delivery or commissioning of new H/W or S/W products occur
Unexpected changes in economic climate alter system objectives	Delays occur in recruitment of key staff	New product documentation proves difficult to penetrate
Personnel changes in user management result in commitment problems	The absorption of new approaches/ products by staff is slower than expected	Product performance falls significantly short of expectations
The organization is restructured causing user responsibility changes	A significant number of tasks prove to be underestimated	Fault identification in multi-supplier configurations proves time consuming
New industrial relations issues arise	Pay and condition problems depress morale	Support by supplier staff proves ineffective

Staff problems

If project slippage can be traced to staff problems then initial thoughts will centre around improving the situation without changing or increasing the manpower deployed. Tasks can be reassigned, closer management with more detailed guidance can be given, emergency training sessions held, and bonuses can be offered. The selected tactic will fit the problem. If, however, these tactics fail then the next step is to alter the use of resources. This may be for quantitative reasons, i.e. the job is proving bigger than was forecast, or for qualitative reasons—the job is proving to be technically too demanding for the staff.

Assigning extra manpower to a project team in an attempt to hold on to a deadline is a tactic which has certain drawbacks. First the new staff will not initially be very productive and they may even diminish the productivity of the original staff who will need to spend time on induction and support. Once this period is over the new larger team has an increased requirement for communication between its various members and may consequently achieve lower individual productivity. It is also unwise to expect a simple arithmetical improvement in output because of the extra staff. It is not true

that five dentists can extract five of your teeth quicker than one working alone. Problem tasks in a systems project may similarly defy a manager's ambition to solve them with increased manpower because they are unsuitable for sub-division. Larger teams also make greater demands on support services and may cause new bottlenecks. Adding extra manpower can be a useful tactic, but it must be introduced early enough for the additional effort to become effective, and it must be small enough, in proportion to the original team, so as not to radically disturb good working relationships.

A consultant with a specific area of expertise can often more rapidly overcome a situation where staff are technically out of their depth. The provision of readily accessible guidance on the use of a new product can bring immediate benefits.

Development tool problems

Perhaps the most intractable problems of all arise from the software or hardware tools chosen to implement the design specification. Staff unfamiliarity or sketchy product documentation can be overcome by training, or close supplier support. Product defects cannot so easily be overcome. It is fortunate if there are any cheap or quick ways out of a problem of this sort. Taking a supplier to court, changing to another supplier, ordering extra or more powerful equipment are all long term solutions which will have little attraction to a project review group which wants a tactic which will be effective in weeks rather than months. There is no satisfaction in being right, possessing a carefully negotiated performance requirement, if a supplier's product proves not to be adequate. Perhaps this is one area where tactical solutions are too late. If project risk is to be minimized then careful evaluation of suppliers and their products must form an important component of the work of the systems development department. In this way confidence is gained in new products prior to their inclusion in system projects.

Implementation of the review resolutions

The project manager will be responsible for implementing the actions identified by a review process. At the lowest level this may involve nothing more than switching tasks between two members of staff. With more significant actions there is also the issue of communication to be considered. Usually there are regular project meetings at which to inform the project team of review actions. For large-scale changes, such as major new user requirements, or equipment changes, a special session should be considered where the project manager can explain the background to the problem, put forward arguments for the alteration and answer any queries.

Another important step is to replan the project. Again, the impact on the current plan will vary enormously. The important issue is that the project must always proceed against a plan which is viable and which reflects the present reality. Otherwise there will be a lack of confidence in plans and an uncertainty which will ultimately undermine the confidence of users and development staff alike.

Replanning will result in amendments to several key items. The project cost summary (Table 5.2) will show a revised estimate which will need to be tabled for agreement at the first available progress review with users and management present. Networks, Gantt Charts and the file of task sheets will also require attention. The benefit of using software packages to achieve this potentially extensive replanning is obvious.

Exercises

1 The time sheet shown in Figure 5.1 represents the traditional means of monitoring projects. As a team leader, identify the ways in which you would use the timesheets of your team members to maintain close monitoring of those aspects of a project for which you are responsible and say what additional information you would seek.

2 List the type of people you would expect to get involved in a monthly project progress review (Level 2, Table 5.1). What agenda would you prepare for such meetings?

3 Give an example of a project for which:
   a) Overspending is acceptable if the time scale is adhered to.
   b) Timescales are not sacrosanct as long as quality is guaranteed.
   c) Quality can be lowered as long as costs are contained.

4 Using the project information shown in Table 5.6 (page 104):
   a) Calculate the efficiency indicators, plot them and comment on the feedback they provide.
   b) What actions might you have recommended to the project review meetings in order that a better performance against plan could be achieved?

5 List the technical and personal attributes which you think are:
   a) necessary

Table 5.6 Project review data

Review number	Original total estimate	Planned manpower consumption (cumulative)	Actual manpower consumed (cumulative)	Manpower content of tasks achieved (cumulative)	Estimate of manpower remaining	Commentary
1	500	100	70	65	435	Project leader called away on maintenance duties
2	500	200	150	120	400	Continued maintenance problems
3	500	300	250	180	350	Project leader now committed, but serious technical problems occur
4	500	400	390	245	280	An extra untrained programmer assigned to project
5	500	500	530	345	210	Project should have been complete. Some difficulties now resolved
6	500	500	630	430	150	Steady progress now achieved
7	500	500	700	500	65	Team size reduced for final stage
8	500	500	770	500	0	Project complete

b) useful
for a person appointed to the role of quality
officer in a systems development department.

Further reading

Golding, D. H., *Project Planning and Control*,
NCC, 1978.

National Computing Centre, *Ensuring Program
Quality*, NCC, 1980.

Parkin, A., *Systems Management*, Arnold, 1980.

6 People management

Introduction

If you talk to anyone about his or her manager, you will hear a list of criticisms. If you ask them about any good managers they have had in their career they may find it possible to pick out, at most, one individual who they reckon to be worthy of consideration. Is it possible that such a high percentage of managers are failing in their jobs? Perhaps the replies have something to do with the natural reticence which employees feel towards extolling the virtues of their superiors. However, a contributory reason is founded in the nature of the management task itself. The roles which a manager must fill are numerous and diverse. A fuller discussion of these roles and their adoption to form styles of leadership is given later. It seems likely, however, that few individuals will be able to shine in each and every one of these roles. At some point in what is otherwise an excellent managerial career there will arise a requirement to adopt a role which does not suit the manager and in which his performance (publicly observed as with most managagement tasks) is not good. The very diversity of the job seems to guarantee that every manager's weaknesses will eventually be found.

The diversity of the task facing the manager during his career means that training and the acquisition of various skills are constantly required. Some of this personal development could and should start early, before any supervisory responsibility is acquired. This helps the young practitioner to understand the objectives and the difficulties of management and develop sympathy for his current manager, and to decide whether such a career would be suitable for him or her. Professional leadership and management courses traditionally make extensive use of group work, including discussions, problem solving and presentations. These courses are popular and frequently improve the motivation of those who attend. They also provide an essential bridge between senior technical proficiency and first thoughts of supervision and leadership. Such a bridge cannot be built by private study alone, and aspirant leaders are recommended to arrange a junior management course as an early part of their self-development programme.

The scope of human factors

In this chapter we are concerned with the human aspects of those who work in computer systems development. Applying knowledge and understanding of these human aspects is an essential part of most of the management process. For example Figure 6.1 (page 106) shows the main influences on the event/action cycle. Some of these are essentially technical (e.g. cost-benefit analysis) and some are concerned with people. The manager must apply this mixture of the social and the technical to each situation. Earlier chapters have dealt with many of the technical considerations of management action. In now considering the social actions and interactions several aspects must be recognized, which arise from the different parties involved. People influence the cycle at three levels.

Personal

The manager must recognize his set of personal views through which various situations that arise are perceived. Additionally he needs to recognize his personal strengths and weaknesses with respect to the different management roles which must be adopted from time to time.

Staff

The manager must understand the general issues which motivate and demotivate staff. However, there may also be specific issues which relate to individual members of staff or to the relationships between them.

Organization

Most organizations have a style or set of expectations with respect to management action which has to be assimilated by a manager. This style will be transmitted by superior and fellow managers and manifest itself in groups such as steering committees and review groups.

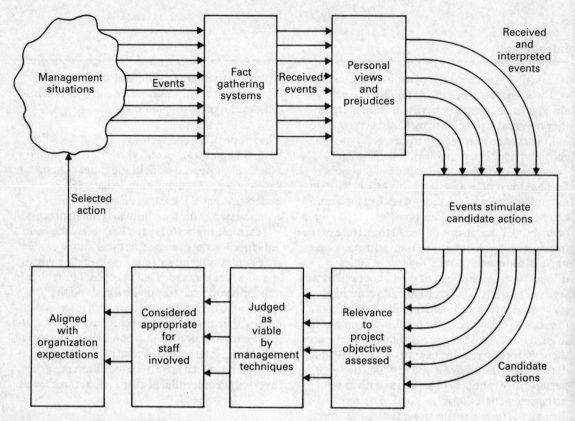

Figure 6.1   *Factors influencing the selection of management action in response to events*

Motivation of staff

Establishing a climate in which system development staff are positively motivated towards their work is a desirable objective for managers and team leaders alike. It will not occur by accident and if a manager is fortunate enough to inherit a good environment then uninformed actions by him could dispel it. It is therefore useful if those who lead, or aspire to lead, understand something of the theories that describe the motivation of staff in general, and the special factors effecting those working in the data processing community in particular.

Theories of motivation are numerous and the area of study from which they have evolved continues to be active. Initial ideas on how people at work were motivated centred on their

productivity. It was held that people worked hard and produced more goods if they were directly rewarded for it. This basic idea led to the establishment of work measurement practices and piece work payment systems. This approach to motivation is retained in many industrial practices where output is directly related to individual efforts. However, the approach is very limiting and has two shortcomings which curtail any general application. First, measuring 'output' is difficult for many classes of people at work, e.g. a fireman or a train driver. In addition, quality of output is important. It would be senseless to pay programmers for each line of COBOL written! Secondly, this method takes no account of other factors which are seen to motivate people because it assumes that the only reward derived from being at work is a financial one.

Before exploring the issues which arise from the second point it is worth noting that one effect of the increased automation of repetitive jobs is to decrease the percentage of jobs susceptible to direct measurement of output. Those who used to earn their income by performing piece work on a lathe are increasingly likely to be involved in setting-up, monitoring and maintaining the service provided by a group of units. Their productivity is thus less clear cut and it becomes even more necessary to explore and utilize a wider range of motivational factors than may have previously been considered.

Job content and individual needs

Once it is recognized that financial reward is not the only factor at play in staff motivation, other contributing factors must be isolated. Herzberg suggested the separation of the motivators from the demotivators, and examples of such factors in a data processing context are shown in Table 6.1.

Table 6.1 Motivators and de-motivators

Motivating factors in the data processing environment	Demotivating factors in the data processing environment
Being allowed to design and construct significant portions of a system with some independence	No clear policy on hardware supplier is evident
Receiving recognition (e.g. given increased responsibility) for work well done	Management allows anomalies (e.g. overtime for maintenance programmers but not other development staff) to flourish
Being booked to attend courses which will introduce new products or methods	Access to hardware for testing purposes is poor
Being made a team leader	There is a history of antipathy between programmers and operators
Being allocated the main update modules in a suite of programs	The absence of a clear information systems strategy fuels speculation about job prospects

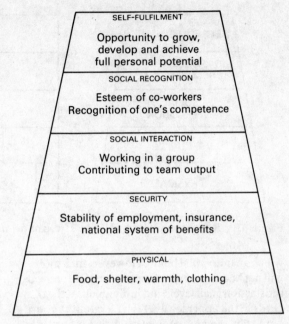

Figure 6.2   *Maslow's Hierarchy of Needs*

The demotivators were dubbed the *hygiene factors* and it was suggested that they represented aspects of a job which it was necessary to get right. Having done so, however, motivation would result only if the motivators were present. In other words the demotivators could break but not make a motivating environment.

Maslow's hierarchy of needs may be seen as a variation of this principle. He defined levels of needs (see Figure 6.2) which interacted in the following way. The lowest levels of need are primary ones which are present in all people and must be satisfied (somewhat equivalent to Herzberg's demotivators). As these lower levels are satisfied then individuals begin more strongly to feel other needs typified by the upper levels in the hierarchy.

For example, most people in employment today have higher expectations of their job than those who were employed in the 1930's. The relative importance (%) of each of Maslow's levels to individuals in these two eras might be something like the pattern of Figure 6.3 (page 108).

Opportunities to satisfy needs at all the levels will, in the first case, be sought within the job

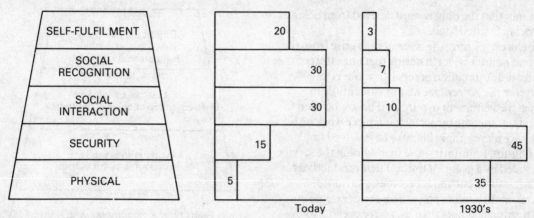

Figure 6.3   *Relative importance of Maslow's levels at two dates*

which an individual holds. However, many jobs will not be able to provide opportunities for needs satisfaction at all levels and individuals with strong needs in the upper levels of the hierarchy who are limited by their job content often find other outlets in sports, hobbies and various social organizations.

The opposite mismatch occurs where individuals feel no strong needs in the upper levels of the hierarchy. In these cases it is not expected that self motivation will ever occur and it would be a mistake to appoint such individuals to jobs that require that kind of commitment.

Other aspects of motivation relate to the reward and punishment of those at work and are based upon the theory of stimulus-response. The study of behaviour in a wide variety of organisms (including people) led to the principle of reinforcement. Applied to work, this suggests that desired behaviour (achieving deadlines, making helpful suggestions) should be rewarded and that undesired behaviour (being late for work, arguing continually with fellow team-members) should be punished. Obviously difficulties will occur when one-sided application of the principles takes place. A reward-oriented manager runs the risk of fomenting poor discipline and eventual disorganization. On the other hand a punishment-orientated manager will quickly establish a cautious attitude among employees which will leave no room for imaginative contributions.

Another aspect of motivation that has to be recognized is the search for equity amongst employees. This is a balance assessed by an employee, first in terms of the contributions made (e.g. experience, education, skill, seniority) against the results achieved (salary, opportunities provided, adverse work factors), thus assessing the *bargain* which that person currently has struck in the job. Secondly the nature of that bargain is compared with other bargains obtained elsewhere by others; in the department, the organization, the profession as a whole and other professions. Groups or individuals strive for equity by seeking to alter the contributions or the rewards of a job so that the bargain is equitable with respect to others. This interest in equity will be important to the personnel department, which needs continually to assess jobs inside and outside the organization to ensure that major discrepancies do not develop. There is likely to be social pressure applied to those whose bargains are not in line with the norm.

Motivation for system development staff

Although system development staff have much in common with other office staff, there is some evidence that their motivational patterns vary slightly and this should lead to specific differences in how they are managed. Couger and Zawacki (*Motivating and Managing Computer Personnel*, Wiley, 1980) have suggested that, in comparison with other staff, systems development workers have a stronger need for personal growth and a weaker need for social involvement. In terms of Maslow's hierarchy (Figure 6.2) they show evidence of need at the highest level – but in some cases seem to miss out in the middle! This relates to the idea of the programmer as a loner, fascinated by the computer, keen to learn more, but unlikely to enjoy progress meetings, user reviews or discussions about quality standards. It is possible to recognize, and channel, the natural inclinations of such a person into a happy and productive role as a programmer. However, if promotion to an analyst's job is sought then this needs pattern may be all wrong. An analyst who avoids social interaction will miss important details about requirements and may unsettle users by his air of apparent indifference.

It would be easy to get these differences out of proportion. Clearly the factors which motivate staff in system development work are similar to those in jobs of equal professional status and interest. Help in the structuring of jobs is to be obtained by looking carefully at these factors and arranging for their recognition in the way that people are directed and developed. Nevertheless it is sensible to incorporate into management some recognition of the distinct motivation patterns of those in systems development work.

Meetings should be arranged carefully as short, structured sessions. The social needs of those participating may become sated by too much directionless discussion.

The concept of the chief programmer team is of interest, but, the low social need factor indicates that the concept should not be taken too far. If we require individuals to channel their production energies only through group efforts and allow too little independent effort then frustration could result for many individuals.

High-achieving programmers with their high growth need are candidates for promotion. Whether or not they are right for a systems analysis role requires a careful assessment of their social skills. Training and counselling can adapt personal attitudes and will improve a person's interactive skills. This approach can solve minor problems. However, the confirmed 'lone programmer' may not wish to adapt, and will therefore seek a career development which continues to supply opportunities for technical growth without increased interaction with people.

Leadership

The requirement for leadership within systems development exists at all levels. In organizations where information systems are vital there will be leadership required from the director of information services to the more junior levels (e.g. team leaders and shift leaders). To be a good leader an individual needs a broad range of different skills. The actions required of a leader can be grouped into a series of roles (see Table 6.2). The skills identified for these roles present a formidable picture of the perfect manager. It is doubtful whether anyone could combine all of these attributes, because some of them are opposites. Even if an individual has a wide range of skills there is the problem of choosing the right ones at the right time, and if a leader adapts his behaviour to suit each situation what will a subordinate make of it – how will anyone know what to expect next? In fact problems of this type rarely occur. In any one leadership situation

certain roles may hardly ever be called upon. The person filling the leadership role is thus required to display a smaller set of skills and can, by judicious delegation, avoid those situations which call for the roles least enjoyed.

Styles of leadership
Setting aside the tasks which arise in leadership, it is useful to look at the *styles* which a leader could employ. By this is meant the approach which the leader adopts towards his subordinates, particularly with respect to their involvement in decision-making and the degree of their interaction with the leader. A useful notion is the *spectrum of styles* (Figure 6.4, page 111) which identifies a continuum of leader/subordinate involvement.

The *director* would weigh alternative solutions to problems – select one and announce it to his subordinates.

Table 6.2   Roles of leadership

Role title	Actions required	Skills needed
Ceremonial	Welcome visitors. Make presentations to leavers.	Public speaking, confidence, wit, tact, sense of humour.
Politician	Represent the function at organization level, major reviews, budget negotiations. Accept responsibility for major successes and failures.	Authority amongst peers. Negotiating and bargaining skills.
Mastermind	Devise a policy for the function. Present and win approval for policy within the organization and the function.	Broad and imaginative thinking retaining a streak of realism. Presentation of a case and response to criticisms.
Planner	Construct detailed plans for acquisition and deployment of people, hardware and software.	Attention to detail. Understanding of the detailed needs of staff, and the technical requirements of computer systems. Ability to handle suppliers.
Administrator	Distribute and monitor tasks, prepare review papers, respond to organization level control requests.	Meticulous approach to paperwork. Administrative skills.
Tactician	Respond to unforeseen events and disturbances to plan. Take advantage of favourable circumstances, such as cut-price equipment deals.	Resourcefulness, level-headedness.
Disciplinarian	Set norms for staff behaviour in work and social terms. Discipline those who consistently fail to recognize these norms.	Ability to set a good example in behavioural terms and to deal firmly with subordinates.
Adviser	Provide guidance on technical matters.	Expertise in a wide variety of technical areas pertinent to the jobs of subordinates.
Counsellor	Listen to subordinate's problems of whatever nature. Encourage and support subordinate. Provide regular feedback to subordinate.	Sympathy, approachability, patience, concern for others.
Inspirationalist	Infuse the objectives of the function with meaning and purpose. Inspire each subordinate to achieve at their highest level.	Enthusiasm, commitment.

The *salesman* would narrow down the options in his search for a solution and then sell to his subordinates the one he favours most.

The *participator* would involve himself with a group of subordinates in an effort to create solutions. He would then participate with that group (probably playing a major role) in selecting the solution considered most appropriate.

The *delegator* would state the problem, possibly define some constraints, and then encourage his subordinates to define and select their preferred solution which would then be adopted.

The *maintainer* would not interfere with subordinates who are expected to identify problems, and create and select solutions as they think appropriate.

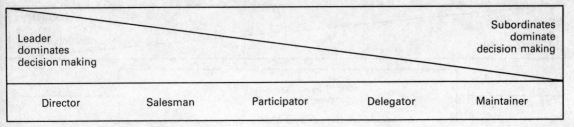

Figure 6.4 *Spectrum of leadership styles*

For any one person the selection of a leadership style may be influenced to some extent by the problem in hand. However, it is more likely that the choice of style will be dictated by forces which relate to the leader himself and to his subordinates. These forces are shown in Figure 6.5 (page 112), and they show how choice of a leadership style moves along the spectrum in response to answers to a series of questions which relate to the value systems of the leader, his confidence in the abilities of his subordinates and the subordinates' own motivation and ambitions.

It is possible to conceive of situations where a style from either end of the spectrum would be appropriate. A section leader asked to start using new trainees will inevitably commence with the style of the director or salesman. By contrast an operations manager with a number of highly experienced systems programmers reporting to him may manage their activities with a low level of involvement equivalent to the delegator or maintainer end of the spectrum.

Leading system development staff

Evidence discussed earlier in this section emphasizes the strong growth need of systems development staff when compared with professional staff of similar status. This suggests they have an interest in exercising control over their own work with minimal interference from their leaders. Perhaps, therefore, the most appropriate forms of leadership in the system development environment are those (participator, delegator, maintainer) which permit such independence. However, other aspects of the situation may not entirely support this conclusion. Staff in systems development have a reputation for being aloof from organizational goals, having in some case a stronger personal commitment to computing as a profession than to their employer. Also having a strong growth need is not the same as being happy to work with unstructured problems. In fact the resolution of a problem is likely to require frequent discussion with others – precisely the kind of activity which those with a low social need would be reluctant to undertake. Selecting a leadership style must therefore take account of these characteristics.

Table 6.3 suggests leadership styles in eight situations dependent upon the levels of growth and social need of subordinates, and the task level. The last factor relates to the nature of the problem being tackled. A task with high characteristics requires significant skill levels, wide skill variety and is seen as being an important piece of work. A task with low characteristics requires a narrow range of low level skills and is seen as being low in importance.

Table 6.3 Leadership styles to suit task and subordinates

	1	2	3	4
Subordinate's:				
Growth need	High	High	Low	Low
Social need	High	Low	High	Low
High task	Delegator	Participator	Salesman	Director
Low task	Participator	Delegator	Delegator	Maintainer

In Column 1 a delegator style is used where task and abilities are both high. Subordinates can satisfy their growth needs by the exercise of

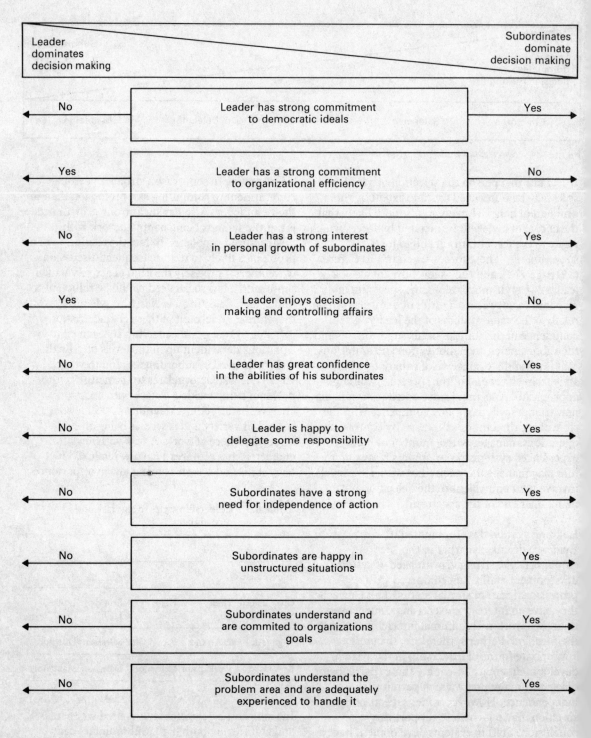

Figure 6.5 *Leadership style selected by leader/subordinate attitude*

discretion over their tasks within some established guidelines. For low tasks more involvement from the leader could help to offset dissatisfaction and maintain support by providing more interaction.

In Column 2 high tasks need a reasonable level of involvement from the leader to ensure that issues are adequately explored by discussion. Low tasks will need less involvement once they are outlined. There is no point in this case in using leader involvement to offset any shortcomings in the task itself.

In Column 3 high tasks need adequate input from the leader to offset a reduced interest in task definition displayed by the subordinates.

However, the social needs factor suggests that interaction would be acceptable and thus a salesman style of leadership would be appropriate. Where the task is low and thus more in line with the subordinate's level of interest, less direction is needed, but interaction would still be appropriate and thus participator or delegator styles would be correct.

In Column 4 a director style would be appropriate to a situation where the leader needs to provide close guidance without a great deal of explanation or interaction. For low tasks the most appropriate style would be the low profile one of maintainer.

Staff development

The appraisal system

One of the greatest services which a manager can perform for the group he leads is to bring clarity to the direction and purpose of their work. The most important action he performs to this end is to translate the overall targets set by senior managers into personal objectives for each member of his group. To work effectively in this way the manager must have the backing of his organization in various ways. First, it helps if the overall policy of the organization is declared and communicated to employees. Secondly, there should be a staff development programme, ideally with the help of the personnel function. Thirdly, there should be a visible organizational commitment to staff development, so that employees can foresee their own personal development and how it will arise.

With this backing a manager responsible for a system development group will be able to operate an effective scheme to clarify targets and to motivate and develop staff in line with their abilities and ambitions. The key to this process is a system of staff appraisal which itself hinges on a periodic appraisal interview. This interview takes place at least annually and should occur between a worker and his or her most immediate supervisor. Such interviews should be instituted at all levels in the organization. Difficulties may arise where the supervisor is considered too junior or

inexperienced to operate the interview correctly and in this case a supervisor higher in the organization would participate in the interviewing process.

The steps involved are shown in Figure 6.6 (page 114). It is usual for a special form to be used to record the various stages of the appraisal process. An example is shown in Figure 6.7 (page 115). The lefthand column (A) is used to create a record of achievement. The righthand column (B) is used to record a plan for the future. Prior to the appraisal interview the appraisee summarizes the activities performed in the last period – reference to section B1 of the previous staff appraisal record is useful here. A special record of difficulties encountered is made. This may include constraints imposed on achievement by inadequate training, hardware difficulties or frequent specification changes. The appraiser has an opportunity to look at these notes prior to the interview and will also prepare himself by reflecting on the overall organization objectives and the way in which the appraisee can assist their achievement.

The appraisal interview itself is a key part of the staff development process and has a unique atmosphere. Perhaps there is no other time when the two people concerned will sit down together with this specific objective of conducting a review of personal achievement and organizing future

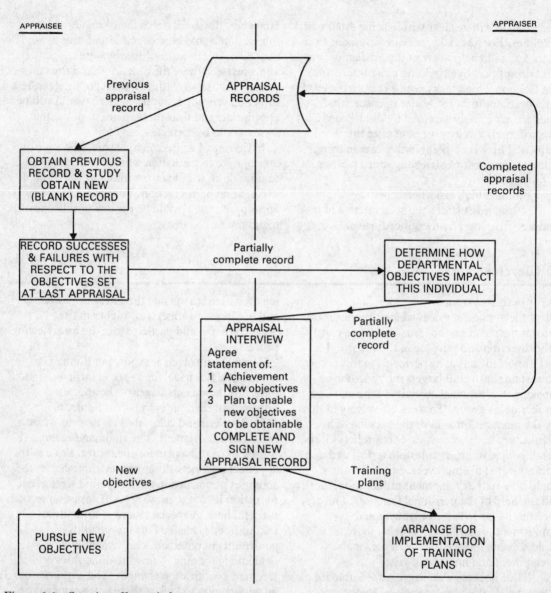

APPRAISEE

APPRAISER

Previous
appraisal
record

APPRAISAL
RECORDS

Completed
appraisal
records

OBTAIN PREVIOUS
RECORD & STUDY
OBTAIN NEW
(BLANK) RECORD

RECORD SUCCESSES
& FAILURES WITH
RESPECT TO THE
OBJECTIVES SET
AT LAST APPRAISAL

Partially
complete record

DETERMINE HOW
DEPARTMENTAL
OBJECTIVES IMPACT
THIS INDIVIDUAL

APPRAISAL
INTERVIEW
Agree
statement of:
1   Achievement
2   New objectives
3   Plan to enable
    new objectives
    to be obtainable
COMPLETE AND
SIGN NEW
APPRAISAL RECORD

Partially
complete
record

New
objectives

Training
plans

PURSUE NEW
OBJECTIVES

ARRANGE FOR
IMPLEMENTATION
OF TRAINING
PLANS

Figure 6.6   *Steps in staff appraisal*

opportunities. The atmosphere should be above all frank without being acrimonious or excessively casual. The appraiser can achieve a great deal by leading the appraisee to look at past work in an objective fashion and perhaps discover some personal weaknesses which have contributed to difficulties. In addition the appraisee's strengths and successes will be brought out and recorded. A joint statement which fairly reflects the discussion (including a note of any differences of opinion) is made to complete this retrospective part of the interview.

The interviewer then uses this understanding to discuss the next period of work. The requirements of the department or section are the basis for defining the appraisee's key objectives

```
┌─────────────────────────────────────────────────────────────────┐
│                                                                   │
│   ┌───────────────────────────────────────────────────────────┐  │
│   │                  STAFF APPRAISAL RECORD                    │  │
│   │  NAME .................. GRADE................. APPRAISER...........│
│   │                                                           │  │
│   │  EMP. NO.................. DEPT.................... DATE OF INTERVIEW ....│
│   └───────────────────────────────────────────────────────────┘  │
│                                                                   │
│   ┌───────────────────────────┐  ┌──────────────────────────────┐ │
│   │ A   RECORD OF ACHIEVEMENT │  │ B   FUTURE OBJECTIVES AND    │ │
│   │                           │  │     DEVELOPMENT PLAN         │ │
│   ├───────────────────────────┤  ├──────────────────────────────┤ │
│   │ A1  APPRAISEE STATEMENT   │  │ B1  KEY OBJECTIVES FOR NEXT  │ │
│   │     OF TASKS PERFORMED    │  │     PERIOD                   │ │
│   │                           │  │                              │ │
│   ├───────────────────────────┤  ├──────────────────────────────┤ │
│   │ A2  APPRAISEE STATEMENT   │  │ B2  LONG TERM CAREER PLAN    │ │
│   │     OF DIFFICULTIES       │  │                              │ │
│   │     ENCOUNTERED           │  │                              │ │
│   ├───────────────────────────┤  ├──────────────────────────────┤ │
│   │ A3  APPRAISER STATEMENT   │  │ B3  FORMAL TRAINING NEEDS    │ │
│   │     OF APPRAISEE          │  │                              │ │
│   │     STRENGTHS AND         │  │                              │ │
│   │     WEAKNESSES            │  │                              │ │
│   ├───────────────────────────┤  ├──────────────────────────────┤ │
│   │ A4  RECORD OF DISCUSSION  │  │ B4  OTHER DEVELOPMENT        │ │
│   │                           │  │     INITIATIVES REQUIRED     │ │
│   │                           │  │                              │ │
│   └───────────────────────────┘  └──────────────────────────────┘ │
│                                                                   │
│   ┌───────────────────────────────────────────────────────────┐  │
│   │  SIGNED BY:- APPRAISEE ............. APPRAISER ............. DATE ..........│
│   └───────────────────────────────────────────────────────────┘  │
│                                                                   │
└─────────────────────────────────────────────────────────────────┘
```

Figure 6.7   *Example staff appraisal record*

(B1 on the record) and the items noted here will reflect the strengths acknowledged in A3. A short time can also be spent on the long term career ambitions of the appraisee and, to the extent that these are relevant to the organization, they may influence the content of B1.

Arising from the appraisal interview, there are a number of actions required to enable the agreed key objectives to be met. Formal courses in techniques or training for management or supervision may be necessary. Other possibilities are changing team membership, arranging secondments or assigning additional responsibilities. These are matters which the appraiser has to implement and they represent the management side of the development bargain. The appraisee's side of the bargain lies in the achievement of objectives which are detailed in section B1 of his appraisal record. It will be easier to achieve and monitor these objectives if they are formulated around precise results. Examples might be:

All program specifications to be implementable in 50 Kbytes.

All system components to be logged in the data dictionary system.

Āchieve error-free listings with two compilation runs.

Turn round maintenance request estimates within 48 hours for 95% of requests.

Reduce absentee rate by 30%.

Training plans

The seriousness with which training is planned depends very heavily on the size of the organization. A small department would treat each requirement for training on its merits and act accordingly. Large organizations have a much greater need. First, they have a continuing requirement for the induction of new staff at every level. This involves providing an organization overview, general policy statements, and introductions to personnel, departmental standards and procedures. In addition those entering at the 'ground floor' may need specific training in the preferred department tools, e.g. COBOL, JSP or Data flow techniques. The continuing nature of these requirements means that instant training techniques such as videos, audio cassettes, booklets and computer-assisted learning packages are often used for the purpose.

Beyond these levels, technical training is required at appropriate points in a person's development (e.g. beginning design responsibilities) or when a new product or technique is adopted by the development department. Having a professional instructor conduct an in-house course is usually less expensive than sending personnel away for training when the numbers involved are greater than five or six. But such courses can be disruptive to the department's work. It is therefore often arranged that key staff are properly trained in certain techniques and they then train other members of the department informally. This has the added benefit of adapting the technique towards the precise needs of the department.

Sometimes training is achieved not by instruction but by carefully planned exposure to new situations. Analysts can often benefit by secondment to user departments. Applications programmers can obtain useful insight by working in a maintenance and user support role. Other managers in the organization may have similar views and development managers may be asked to provide placements for young accountants, engineers or marketing staff.

Training for supervisory roles needs very careful planning and will be sensitive to the needs of individuals. Some form of assessment may be needed at first, to gauge a candidate's suitability for supervisory work. Training to identify and address personal characteristics (e.g. poor public speaking, deficient interpersonal skills) may be needed. Periods of practice of supervisory work interspersed with periods of training can then build up a person's management capability by ensuring that not only is a certain technique assimilated but that the need for it is also experienced and understood.

One further type of training is undertaken by system development departments and it is associated with those personnel whose objectives include the development of new techniques and products. These people, charged with the research and development role, have the open objective of keeping abreast of relevant developments. They will need to keep in contact with academics, with manufacturers and with the initiatives being undertaken by other system development departments, particularly those in competitor organizations. Attendance at seminars, user groups and product launches is necessary. They must summarize and disseminate the information gleaned so that others can contribute to assessing the relevance of the new ideas. This type of training is usually arranged for systems development managers, including senior technical supervisors.

Recruitment

Recruitment arises in response to expansion plans and as a result of staff turnover. The computing industry has been operating for many years in an environment where both occur rapidly, and so in system development, recruitment is a permanent feature of a manager's life. In large departments a policy of trainee intake recognizes the tendency for more experienced staff to move on, and therefore seeks to maintain a constant flow of staff through the various experience levels. The first step in the recruitment process is therefore to plan to avoid it by aligning a developing individual with each post. This will inevitably fail at some point, so that recruitment at above the trainee level becomes necessary. The key preparatory step for this recruitment is to establish precise knowledge of the job specification, and of the type of person needed to do it. Examples of these specifications are shown in Table 6.4.

The manager concerned will have these specifications to hand as essential parts of the supervisory process. The details would be checked immediately prior to recruitment. Perhaps in the case of a job which involves a considerable degree of involvement with user staff it may be beneficial to involve a key user in creating or adjusting the specifications.

There is the possibility that a preference for internal recruitment exists within the

Table 6.4 Job specification and person specification

Job specification	Person specification
Job title	Normally suitable age range
Company grade	
Salary scale	Normally required standard of general education
Normal preceding job title	
Normal succeeding job title	Normally required length of experience
Prerequisite skills and knowledge on entry to job	Personal attributes required
Main duties and responsibilities	
Subsidiary duties and responsibilities	Mobility and flexibility required
Responsible to whom	
Responsible for whom	
Conditions of work	
Normal place of work	

organization. This ensures that current employees are given every opportunity to further their careers. Individuals from outside the system

Table 6.5 Advantages and disadvantages of recruiting from within the organization

Advantages	Disadvantages
The recruitment process is cheaper.	Aptitude of internal recruit for training and new work difficult to assess.
The recruit is generally available more quickly.	
No need to acquire company knowledge.	An outsider with precisely the right required skills could deliver benefits more quickly.
Reduces domestic upheaval and resultant interference with work.	
Character/personality of recruit will be well known.	An outsider with a fresh approach could stimulate the department.
Recruit could bring valuable user knowledge into the development environment.	The transferred recruit may hang on to old allegiances and fail to develop new ones.

development department may apply and be suitable for trainee positions, or possibly for retraining for a business analysis role. Internal recruitment has much to recommend it (see Table 6.5) and should never be ignored.

Advertising, interviewing and selection

It is important to recognize the likely timescale involved in recruiting an outsider. Table 6.6 shows a typical timescale. Thereafter a settling period would be needed, to adapt to the new standards required and to establish personal relationships. If manpower needs are urgent, contract labour is a better solution.

Advertising for staff should involve the services of a professional, either an agency or an in-house personnel function. Buying sufficient space to include all the job details will probably be too expensive, and so a shortened but pertinent and attractive description is needed. Personnel agencies can be used if initial anonymity is required or a heavy response is expected. These agencies are capable of undertaking a great deal of the time consuming work associated with recruitment and can reduce the effort needed by the department to a single day's interviewing of the shortlisted candidates.

Table 6.6 Timescale for personnel recruitment

Recruitment tasks	Typical time needed
Revise and agree job and person specifications with interested parties	5 days
Arrange for advertisements to appear	7 days
Allow for closing date	10 days
Shortlist formed	3 days
Invite for interview and allow interviewees to reply and to attend	8 days
Interview, offer and acceptance	10 days
Period of notice worked by recruit	30 days
	10 weeks

If the entire selection is to be undertaken unaided then initial selection will be based upon the statements made in the application form. The extent to which they match the job and person specifications is the main basis for selection. The clarity and perception of any free-format statements made on the form will also help to narrow the field. The ideal short list is probably between three and seven. The selected candidates should have their references taken up and be offered interview dates. Ideally all candidates should be interviewed together, with a view to a decision being taken on that day. The structure of the interview day can take a variety of forms but the main objectives are:

1 To decide which candidates, if any, are acceptable for the post advertised.
2 To decide which of the candidates satisfying the above criterion is the best choice for the post.

The first objective will have been reasonably well achieved by studying the application forms, but the interview day is the opportunity to confirm the statements which the forms contain. The second objective requires the selection of the candidate who:

Has the skills and knowledge required for the job

Is likely to enter into team relationships which are positive

Has grasped and appears committed to the job specification

In balancing these requirements it may happen that the candidate who appears the most skilled or knowledgeable is passed over for one of lesser technical achievement who offers more certainty of settling into the job and contributing to the team effort.

In order to satisfy these objectives and assess candidates for the various attributes in which there is interest, the interview day is designed to include certain components. A structure of the interview day is shown in Table 6.7.

Table 6.7   Structure of an interview day

	Component	Objective of component
1	Candidate sent programme for day, including details of any special preparation they should undertake (e.g. making a short presentation).	To give candidates opportunity to demonstrate their personal standards of work in terms of their preparatory material.
2	Introductory talk from a manager giving top-down view of organization which sets the context for this job and describes it and the conditions of service in detail.	To inform candidates and ensure that no misunderstandings about long term objectives or the precise nature of the duties arise.
3	Interview by a manager with appropriate technical competence.	To examine and evaluate the candidate's CV with respect to the depth of the experience and skills described. To allow the candidates to explore questions they may have regarding the job or its context.
4	Possible appraisal of competence e.g. – short test on COBOL – explain a schema – make a short presentation	To obtain direct evidence of the candidate's skill in a specific task.
5	Each candidate (either singly or as a group) meets potential team-mates from the organization in an informal atmosphere (e.g. a coffee-break).	Allows the social skills of the candidates to be demonstrated and permits potential team-mates the opportunity to observe and comment on the individual candidates.
6	Evidence from initial sessions is gathered and some ranking or categorizing of candidates is performed.	At this stage the favourites will have emerged. If the interview arrangements are spread over two days probably only these few will return for the second day. Otherwise the final stages are undertaken in the light of the findings.
7	Panel interview.	To make a final selection by obtaining answers to questions raised in the previous stages and by possibly adjusting the ranking accordingly.
	Panel members	
	Immediate manager.	Present to represent interest in the competence and suitability of the individual employed and to help communicate the outcome of the previous stages.
	More senior manager.	Similar to above but with a wider and longer term view.
	A manager from another part of the organization.	Provides a lateral view. May represent user interests and be present to help implement any relevant computer steering committee policy matters.
	A member of the personnel function.	Ensures appointments are made in accordance with organizational employment rules.

In varying these components it is important to retain the two-way nature of the interview process. Candidates must be given sufficient opportunity to understand the organization, the job specification and the personal requirements so that if an offer is made, it can be accepted confidently and with commitment.

Exercises

1 Explain how the concept of a project team helps individuals to satisfy needs in the upper levels of Maslow's hierarchy (Figure 6.2). In what ways might the requirement to work in a team frustrate the satisfaction of needs?

2 To what extent do you think the relatively large demand for, and consequent shortage of, system development staff contributes to the difference in motivation between them and other types of professional worker which has been noted by Couger and Zawacki?

3 Using the named leadership styles from Figure 6.4 identify and justify your choice of a style in each of the following situations:
   a) A new system development manager wishes to gain rapid acceptance for some sort of program design technique (currently no standard exists) among the programming team leaders.
   b) As part of a reorganization a system development manager has to create an information centre from existing staff and this involves 'robbing' his project leaders of some of their staff.
   c) A new quality officer has been appointed and has some novel but promising ideas. The system development manager sees that they will need to be defined to a level of detail acceptable to project leaders.

4 Identify particular problems which you would expect to arise in the following appraisal situations:
   a) A young, able, newly promoted project leader has to appraise an older and somewhat stolid senior programmer.
   b) A senior programmer is appraising a programmer recently joined straight from college.
   c) A system development manager is appraising an experienced project leader who will probably not go further.

5 When asked about recruitment, managers will often confirm that the principal requirement they have is that a recruit should show evidence of ability to work in a team. Why is this so important? How does the interview process (Table 6.7) look for this ability? What are the dangers of concentrating too heavily on this abilit

Further reading

Chadd, L. J., Naughton, M. J. B., Jebay, B., *The Team Approach in Data Processing*, Input Two Nine, 1978.

Chandor, A., *Choosing and Keeping Computer Staff*, Allen and Unwin, 1976.

Couger, J. D., Zawacki, R. A., *Motivating and Managing Computer Personnel*, Wiley 1980.

Mumford, E., *Job Satisfaction–A Study of Computer Specialists*, Longman 1972.

Weinberg, G. M., *The Psychology of Computer Programming*, Van Nostrand, 1971.

7 Implementation, maintenance and audit

Introduction

Successful systems spend the majority of their lives in the hands of their users. After the relatively brief period of incubation known as development, systems are first implemented and subsequently operated by users who obtain support and guidance from the data processing department as required. The management task related to these activities is, therefore, to plan and oversee a smooth transition of the system into a publicly operational state and, thereafter, to maximize the benefits from the implemented system by working with the users to monitor and adjust its performance.

Implementation, as defined here, refers to the transition of a system from construction to live use. Project teams will have been in close contact with at least some of the intended users throughout the life of the project. The level of this contact tends to vary depending on the size of the contribution to the project which users are actually making. This is illustrated in Figure 7.1

and shows that the move from construction to implementation represents a turning point in a project as user interest begins to step up. User involvement during construction has centred around joint reviews of cost and progress. Also they will have participated in demonstrations of each element of the system as completion takes place. At the beginning of the implementation phase, user interest quickens and eventually dominates the project. Implementation will be deemed completed at some carefully defined end point and the early stages of operation will commence with development staff offering close support and a rapid response to problems.

The management of this transition from the hectic but restricted activities of final programming and testing to the public stage of acceptance tests and training, calls for careful review of the inherent problems. The first is that development staff may have lost sight of the overall objective of the system in their attention to

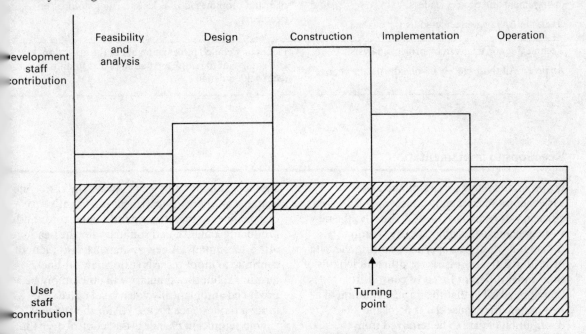

Figure 7.1 *Comparative contribution of user and development staff over lifecycle*

detail. Secondly, the circle of users involved with the system must be widened quickly and effectively. Thirdly, management commitment to the system must now be demonstrated. Fourthly, it is likely that minor inconsistencies and misunderstandings may now come to light, together with a few problems of a more substantial kind. Finally, a difficult path must be steered between responding to user feedback on the one hand and maintaining project momentum on the other.

It is clear that there is need to inform, interest and commit the greater audience which now exists for the system. Events which could achieve this *awakening* objective are defined in Table 7.1.

It is a mistake to assume that because a certain group of people appear not to be affected they need not be told about a new system. A development team should create as positive an atmosphere as possible, and neutral people are much more likely to be well-disposed towards the system if they are kept informed.

The level of cooperation between developer and user is crucial in ensuring that the implementation phase proceeds as smoothly as possible. Where the project is very small and informal this cooperation may be easy. Other situations may be more difficult, for example where the development team and the user group are large, or the relationship between them is very formal. In these circumstances cooperation will be favoured by a well-defined implementation plan.

Table 7.1   Events to announce the implementation plan

Event	Objective
General announcement e.g. house journals. *Audience*: The whole organization	Informs the widest possible audience about the new investment in systems.
Presentation of implementation plan by senior management and project leaders. *Audience*: Any person effected by the change	Demonstrates high level commitment, communicates plan and promotes feedback concerning unforeseen problems.
Technical seminars given by project analysts. *Audience*: All those closely involved with the change	Passes on detailed information about the operation and control of the implementation plan. Obtains feedback on details.

Reactions to implementation

Information systems are implemented for a variety of reasons, mainly concerning increased efficiency or responsiveness. Typically, the new systems achieve this objective by creating different flows of data, perhaps causing the data to be held in different places for different lengths of time under different forms of control. It is therefore possible that the implementation of a new system may cause the control and distribution of data to be removed from the responsibility of one group of people and given to another, although this is not always the case. One example is where a department is currently responsible for maintaining financial records and producing a month-end summary for the head office accountant. A new system may ask them to continue to input records (using new on-line terminals) but the summary will now simply be produced automatically when head office staff input a request (see Figure 7.2 for the change).

One significant change is that control over the timing and selectivity of the report has been lost

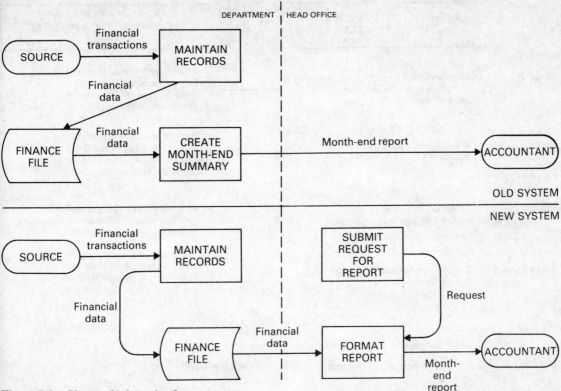

Figure 7.2   *Change of information flow*

by the departmental staff and now resides with head office. Previously, departmental staff would have exercised discretion over what details were included in the report, they may even have slightly delayed its production to allow for late arrivals. Now this 'gate-keeping' power will be lost.

There are many instances where the power exercised by people (groups or individuals) derives from the control they exercise over the storage and dissemination of data. For this reason every change to an information system is potentially a disturbance to the power relations in an organization, and wherever it has been designed that some power is transferred from one group to another, one can expect resistance from the potential losers. Of course these issues are likely to have been raised and resolved much earlier, perhaps during the feasibility study.

Resistance to change can take many forms. One tactic is the ostrich approach, which tries to ignore change. Another is not to show one's hand until implementation starts. Then sufficient prevarication and unenthusiastic cooperation can neutralize the impact of change and help retain the status quo. Or the ostensibly enthusiastic group may request one enhancement after another to delay the acceptance of the new system.

The existence of these tactics argues for careful consideration and construction of an implementation plan. A glance at some data flow diagrams (such as those in Figure 7.2) will identify likely power shifts and potential resistance centres. If there is suspicion that some groups will oppose implementation, then the project leader can act to ensure that problems are aired openly and quickly. This will be achieved by personal rather than written communication, perhaps in meetings, where commitment is asked for and difficulties are forced into the open. The resolution of a major problem is likely to require the services of a senior management

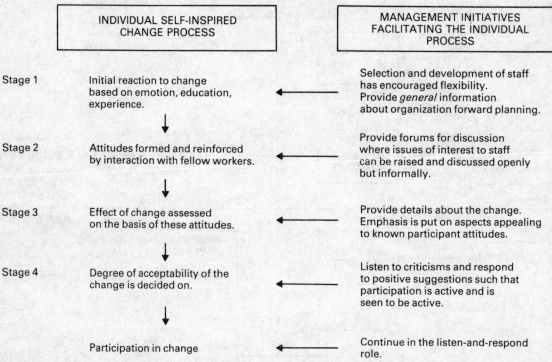

| INDIVIDUAL SELF-INSPIRED CHANGE PROCESS | MANAGEMENT INITIATIVES FACILITATING THE INDIVIDUAL PROCESS |

Stage 1 — Initial reaction to change based on emotion, education, experience. ← Selection and development of staff has encouraged flexibility. Provide *general* information about organization forward planning.

Stage 2 — Attitudes formed and reinforced by interaction with fellow workers. ← Provide forums for discussion where issues of interest to staff can be raised and discussed openly but informally.

Stage 3 — Effect of change assessed on the basis of these attitudes. ← Provide details about the change. Emphasis is put on aspects appealing to known participant attitudes.

Stage 4 — Degree of acceptability of the change is decided on. ← Listen to criticisms and respond to positive suggestions such that participation is active and is seen to be active.

Participation in change ← Continue in the listen-and-respond role.

Figure 7.3   *Management participation in an individual-inspired change process*

representative who can conduct realistic negotiations, and offer solutions which can genuinely be delivered.

It must be emphasized that the best way of avoiding difficulties at this late stage is to begin the project in as open and frank a manner as possible, providing extensive opportunities for all participants to contribute to the evolution of the system. If this is done then there is considerably less opportunity for disruptive tactics by any party.

The change process itself needs to be carefully analysed. Initiatives should be undertaken which will facilitate each component of a change. Management influence over the change process may be considered to be *directive*. However, if one looks at the process by which individuals might themselves incline towards and participate in change, then the role for management direction may be to stimulate rather than demand this inclination. Figure 7.3 shows the stages which an individual goes through in responding to and participating in a change process. Examples of management initiatives relevant to each stage are also shown which illustrate how management participation in this change process can work by encouraging positive individual discoveries rather than by simply taking a lead and asking the participants to follow. Once this approach has been successfully used for one change it is to be hoped that a positive climate is established in which any sensible change can be confidently expected to occur.

User preparation

Two groups of tasks are necessary before the actual changeover to the new system can commence. One group is associated with acceptance, the other group with training. Which

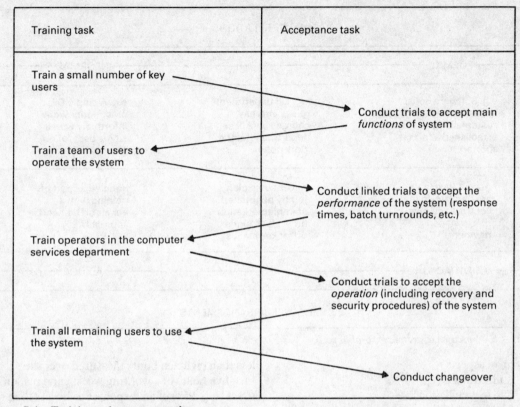

Training task	Acceptance task
Train a small number of key users	Conduct trials to accept main *functions* of system
Train a team of users to operate the system	Conduct linked trials to accept the *performance* of the system (response times, batch turnrounds, etc.)
Train operators in the computer services department	Conduct trials to accept the *operation* (including recovery and security procedures) of the system
Train all remaining users to use the system	Conduct changeover

Figure 7.4   *Training and acceptance tasks*

comes first? The quandary is that users will not be able confidently to agree to the acceptance of the system unless they have received sufficient training to operate it! Solutions to this quandary are usually negotiated by interleaving the acceptance and training tasks. Figure 7.4 illustrates how this could be arranged.

Acceptance trials

The degree of formality attached to acceptance trials is defined by the relationship between the developers and the users. A spectrum of formality could be defined as in Figure 7.5. Factors such as the extent to which there is a strict commercial arrangement between users and developers influences the arrangements for acceptance trials. In the case of a development conducted by an external software house for a user organization, users will want to ensure that they understand what is being delivered and be confident that it

meets stated requirements. The suppliers of the system will want to ensure customer satisfaction, avoiding a flurry of late, uncosted additions to the negotiated agreements. Long before the system is delivered, negotiations should commence to define the nature of the acceptance trials. In this most formal of situations the structure and content of the trials should be precise. The areas which the user will want to look at are listed below:

Functional aspects
   The transactions
   The enquiry responses
   The output formats
   The integrity of the data base

Performance aspects
   Response times
   Batch job run times
   Time between failures
   Proportion of time system is available

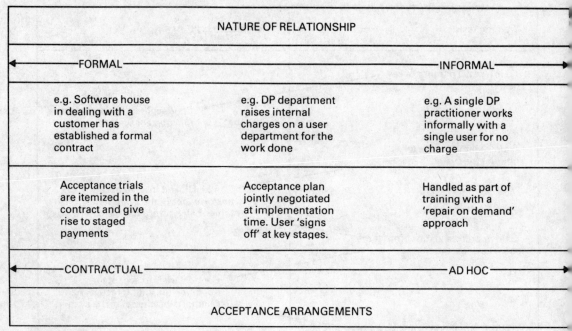

Figure 7.5   *Spectrum of acceptance trial formality*

Control aspects
  Audit trails
  File reconciliations

Operational aspects
  Main and secondary storage use
  Security tasks
  Restarts and recovery procedures

The negotiation between user and developer is conducted on the basis of agreeing what is measurable and acceptable in each of the categories above. The developer will wish to build some flexibility into the acceptance procedures and the user must therefore think rationally and objectively about what is needed. For example, an attempt to stipulate that the system be available 'at all times' would be doomed to misinterpretation. A more precise requirement would be that the availability of the system would be such that all user functions were available for 98% of the elapsed time between 0800 and 1900 hours in the five days of a normal working week. Similar statements should set targets for failure rates (e.g. with a mean time between failure of not less than eighteen hours measured over the fifty-five hours of a working week), and response times (e.g. 95% of all responses to be less than or equal to three seconds, measured from depression of the ENTER button to the return of the last character of response to the screen), and for all other quantifiable aspects of the system.

Once this definition has taken place (the roots are, of course, back in the feasibility study and the design criteria for the system), it remains for the user to mobilize sufficient trained staff to conduct the tests, and for the developers to deliver the actual system and its documentation. Users should be prepared to test the system realistically and comprehensively during the trial periods. The tests will require:

An overall acceptance test schedule.

Sets of realistic test data linked to form complete cycles (weeks, months, years).

Measurement devices (e.g. stop watches) and performance recording formats.

Means of quickly and conveniently recording results and any other unexpected events (screen printers, cameras, utilities to copy and compare files).

A list of controlled calamities to which the system will be exposed in order that restart and recover procedures can be assessed.

A mechanism for reviewing the results of the trials has to be arranged with the developers too – in the form of a series of formal minuted reviews where events which have occurred in the trials are notified and discussed. Each of these events goes through a series of evolutionary stages.

Discussion
The event is given official status (logged into the review system) and therefore the user can expect the problem to be 'chased' until an explanation is found. Alternatively the event may be considered unimportant and ignored.

Classification
The logged events are classified according to importance and urgency. A numerical indicator may be applied (see Table 7.2).

Table 7.2   Event classes

Event class	Action
1	Undertake investigation and incorporate solution at a convenient point
2	Solution should be incorporated in next major release
3	Solution should be urgently sought and implemented in the current release
4	The event gives rise to serious problems which require the dedication of all possible resources
5	Trials are suspended and cannot proceed until a solution is found

Resource
Considering all of the events registered, resources are allocated according to the classification of the events.

Review
At successive reviews progress on each event is discussed. The event may be formally declassified, or have its classification revised up or down.

This system for event handling ensures that nothing significant which occurs in the trials is neglected and that resources are utilized as effectively as possible. Ultimately the system is managed through these reviews, to the next stage of the implementation phase (which could be full user staff training or live changeover). However, it is possible that this set of trials will need to be mounted on future occasions, e.g. after a significant amount of maintenance work. It is worth documenting the whole package of procedures and data to permit its rapid reuse on these occasions.

Training
Training user staff to understand and take advantage of the newly implemented system is an activity which is the responsibility of those leading the development project, i.e. user managers and senior system development staff. A strategy for training involves deciding between various options.

Sequence
Who should be trained first, management or operational staff?

Timing
Is the training to be concentrated in a short spell just before changeover, or will it be spread over a longer period?

Personnel
Will the training be by professional trainers, development staff, a dedicated group of user staff, or will it be allowed to 'trickle' down between each level of user staff?

Method
Should the training be carried out by lecture, video, informal hands-on sessions, or individual instruction?

Tactical considerations may dictate some of these choices, but certain characteristics of the project play a major part in deciding the training strategy. Most important are the characteristics of the target staff. Users who have no experience of the proposed type of system will make greater demands of the training schedule. Older users (at all levels) often lack confidence with computer systems and may resent being asked to learn new skills. It may be considered inappropriate for a young systems analyst to instruct senior managers so protocol is important. Staff may be unsure of the benefit the system will bring to their own particular job and thus show a lack of commitment.

The strategy of who trains who, for how long and by what method will be heavily influenced by recognition of these user characteristics. Also the objectives which a user pursues in future contacts

with the proposed system vary considerably and the type of training needed to qualify the user to pursue these objectives will differ in intensity and content. Table 7.3 gives an example of users, their objectives, and appropriate training.

In implementing training plans a wide variety of methods is available. The first is via the *system itself*. If the induction of new staff can regularly be expected over the life of the system then a training mode can be built in at the design stage. This would have special features such as extensive help facilities, and the use of non-live files.

Audio/visual programmes may be useful for several widely spread groups of users. One advantage which these techniques offer is the control which the learner can exercise.

Table 7.3   User staff and appropriate training

Staff level	Staff objectives in their contacts with the system	Training method
Senior management	To monitor the extent to which the system delivers its intended benefits.	Seminars giving system overview with examination of intended benefits and how they will be obtained.
Middle management	To control the system, deal with exceptions and modify rules and procedures in the event of the system becoming inaccurate or unwieldy. To benefit from summary information produced by the system.	Seminar giving overview of system management. Individual sessions on interpretation of audit outputs and periodic reports.
User operational staff directly concerned with the system	To operate, accurately and efficiently, input, processing, data storage, retrieval and output procedures.	Seminar giving overview of system objectives. Appropriate form of detailed hands-on session with small user groups. Time for practice should be allowed. The early establishment of some of these users as local experts is helpful.
Computer service operations staff	To operate the computer procedures required for the system. To secure data and enact efficiently recovery procedures.	Seminar giving system overview. Walkthrough of all computer procedures.
Development staff	To maintain and enhance the system in response to user requirement.	System overview seminar. Technical presentation on design features.
User staff not closely associated with the system	To understand the reason for the system and be familiar with its main features.	System overview seminar given by those users most involved in the implementation.

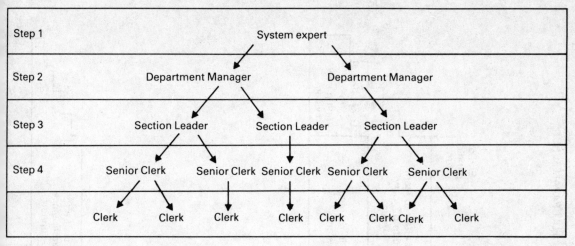

Figure 7.6 *An example of trickle training*

Trickle training is a method whereby training can be proliferated among a large number of operators using a sort of pyramid technique as in Figure 7.6. Apart from being an efficient use of expert knowledge, the technique has the advantage that it does not require the system expert to communicate with all of the people involved. This cuts out jargon problems and promotes situations where local terminology and appropriate emphasis are used.

Formal presentations are best when short (20–40 minutes) and used to give the audience an overview of an area. Communicating more detailed information is best achieved by providing documents for private study or individual tuition. Having an obvious structure to the presentation is a useful way of letting the audience know for how much longer they have to sit still, and a closing summary is a good opportunity to emphasize the main points of the talk. Good visual aids are extremely useful in keeping the audience's interest, as is the tactic of having more than one speaker.

Changeover

The act of changeover from an old system to a new system can often make the heaviest instantaneous demands on development and user resources. It is even possible to imagine situations where consideration of the complexity and

expense of just this act can tip the feasibility decision against an otherwise attractive proposal. The first main point is to ensure that all preparations are complete. A project network will provide a checklist to work from. The areas to check are:

The system – programs, jobs, documents, manuals.

The users – training, acceptance, commitment.

The equipment – mainframe, micros, terminals, communications networks.

The plan – what are the steps for the changeover?

Changeover plans vary in abruptness from the 'Big Bang' approach, which asks users to pick up a new system while simultaneously dropping the old, to the gentler full parallel run approach which requires users to operate both systems for some time. Taking these two extremes, it should be noted that the pattern of their consumption of resources and the purposes they serve are different. Resource usage variations are shown in Figure 7.7 (page 130). The Big Bang approach is actually more structured with essential activity completed before changeover. Other approaches tend to rely on training and acceptance trials

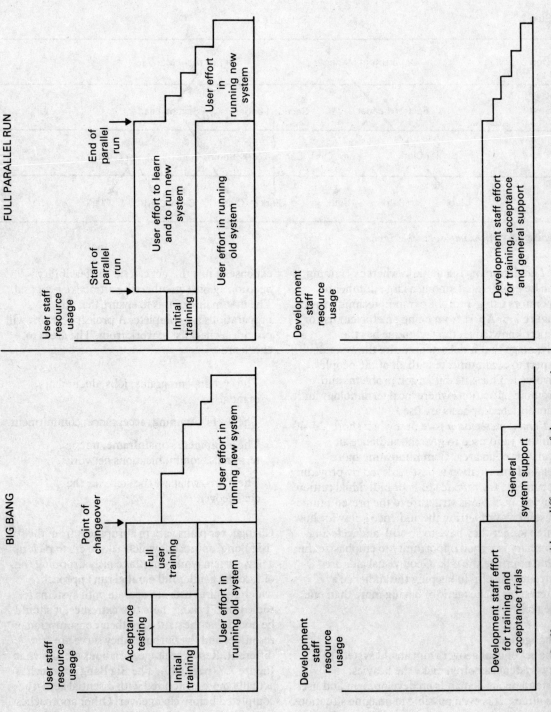

Figure 7.7   *Staff resource usage with two different types of changeover plan*

proceeding together until the old system can confidently be dropped.

Many hybrid plans can be devised which lie between these extremes.

1 A single section of the user department can conduct parallel runs which gradually build confidence to the point where the rest of the user department can change over with a Big Bang.
2 A series of 'Mini Bangs' can be devised wherever a system or its users can be clearly compartmentalized.

3 A preliminary pilot study can be used to decide whether a full scale Big Bang is feasible, or whether a phased plan is necessary.

Generally more user resource is required over longer periods when parallel plans are devised. If a user department relies heavily on a system then the full parallel running of two (the old and the new) is not likely to be sustainable for long periods. In these situations, strong arguments exist for a carefully structured build-up, including properly devised acceptance trials and thorough preparatory training.

System maintenance

In many D.P. departments, the effort spent on maintaining a system exceeds all the effort spent in the earlier phases of developing that system. Figure 7.8 shows typical amounts of effort put in at various stages during the life of a system.

Maintenance gradually becomes more important as an organization becomes more

mature in its use of computers and begins to proliferate information systems within its various functions. Figure 7.9 (page 132) shows how, in an environment where there is a build up in systems development activity, the effort applied to maintenance eventually rises to be a very significant proportion of total systems development activity.

This chart assumes that systems have a life of five years and shows how in the steady state (dictated perhaps by a limit on the D.P. budget or staff numbers) the maintenance work load would exceed development work. The situation becomes worse if development activity, including the replacement of old systems, is neglected. As systems become more and more modified, they become harder to maintain, and consume greater and greater amounts of development resource. A sluggish policy of system replacement could lead to the kind of balance shown in Figure 7.10 where maintenance work has exploded out of control.

Maintenance management and control
Some maintenance requirements arise from errors and misunderstandings in the original specification of the system. If good development standards have been observed these should not consume significant resources. However, there are other causes of maintenance requirements:

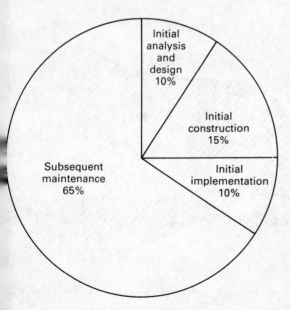

Figure 7.8 *Effort expended on a system during its life*

Statutory changes (esp. in payroll systems)

Economic changes

Competition (new reporting requirements)

New management (changed timetables)

Altered reporting structures

New hardware has to be absorbed (JCL reformatted)

New software adopted (file use re-considered).

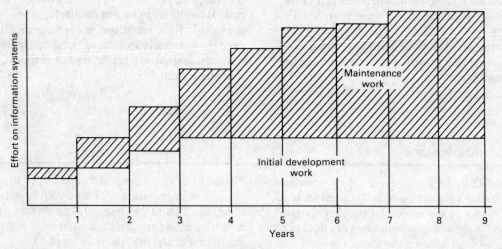

Figure 7.9   *Growth in maintenance as systems are implemented*

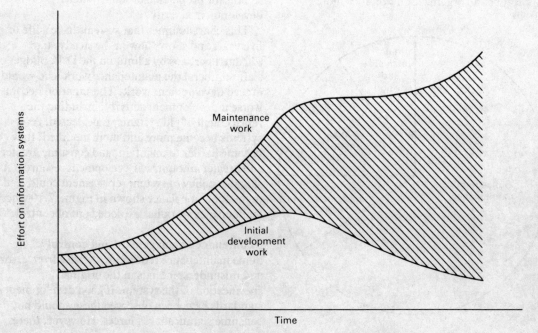

Figure 7.10   *Surge of maintenance work resulting from inadequate system replacement*

Scale of maintenance requirement / Development phase	Major enhancement	Additional reporting needs	Absorb H/W or S/W changes	Minor error fix
Feasibility	X			
Requirement study	X	X		
Design	X	X	X	
Specification	X	X	X	X
Construction	X	X	X	X
Integration	X	X	X	X
Implementation	X	X	X	X

Figure 7.11   *Project structure defined by scale of maintenance requirement*

This list should look familiar. In fact these are the very forces that stimulate feasibility studies in the first place! Thus maintenance work requires the same sort of project management and control as full scale projects. Of course the size of the maintenance job dictates the extent to which all of the usual phases are employed.

Figure 7.11 gives an indication of how the scale of a maintenance requirement directs the structure of the project. Large projects requiring feasibility and requirement studies are easily absorbed into the project management and control environment of strategic systems development (see Chapter 3). Smaller maintenance jobs present a different set of problems which probably need a specific administrative system.

One of the unique features for small scale maintenance jobs is the need to perform rapid (perhaps automated) but comprehensive system level tests before the amended system replaces the old version. This set of operations is critically important and requires careful definition and control.

During the initial development of all systems a well-documented *test-set* should be built up. This will consist of a fully representative transaction set, a realistic database and expected results in the form of master copies of reports, enquiry responses and control outputs.

The test-set is valuable and will require updating as the system and its data evolve. Extra confidence in testing amendments is obtained if a very recent database is used.

If it is necessary for a single member of staff to perform a high volume test, the existence of an automated proving system (having file comparison programs, generalized enquire/print programs, totalling and other data manipulation utilities) is desirable.

The control exercised over the labelling of programs and their copying from maintenance to a live directory must be extremely tight. Live directories should have a highly protected status and writing into them is best reserved for one or two senior hands. A control form recording the transfer is a useful discipline.

Maintenance request approval
At some point in the life of a system (normally at the end of changeover) an agreement is reached between developers and users that the system is

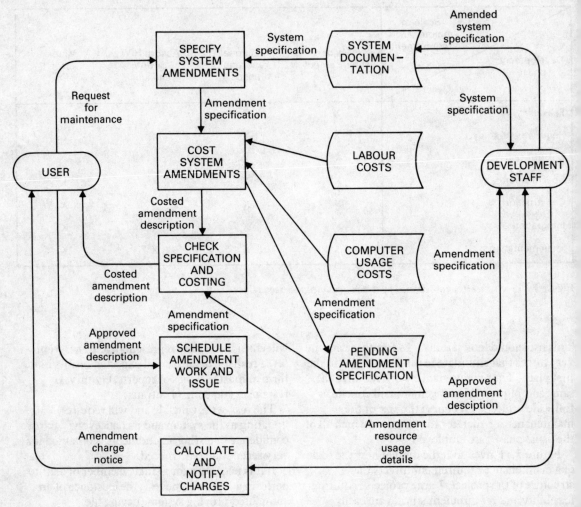

Figure 7.12 *Charge-out for maintenance work*

delivered and all future work will be based upon maintenance requests. The mechanism for controlling these requests is fundamentally dependent upon the way in which the systems development department reports within the organization. If the department charges users for work done and is required to turn in a breakeven or profit performance, then a system of request costing and mutual approval will exist. If no charging out is done then a simple queue of requests is formed. Request priorities must then be negotiated and agreed between the systems development manager and a user group – perhaps

in the form of a junior computer steering committe

A maintenance request procedure is shown in Figure 7.12 and Figure 7.13 shows an example of a control document which would guide maintenance requests during their life. The assumption so far is that charges are derived from the actual work completed. Development staff may however, find themselves in the slightly sharper environment of having to achieve system amendments against a fixed price quotation.

The arguments for and against charging users for maintenance work are similar to those used for charging in the wider systems development

```
┌─────────────────────────────────────────────────────────────────┐
│                    SYSTEM MAINTENANCE CONTROL                     │
│                                          SERIAL NO. . . . . . . .  │
│  ┌──────────────────────────────────────────────────────────┐   │
│  │ A  AMENDMENT REQUEST                                      │   │
│  │      DIVISION/DEPT . . . . . . . . . . USER/ACCOUNT CODE. . │   │
│  │      SYSTEM(S) REQUIRING AMENDMENT  . . . . . . . . . . . . │   │
│  │      DESCRIPTION OF AMENDMENT (USE ADDITIONAL SHEETS AS NEEDED) │
│  │                                                           │   │
│  │                                                           │   │
│  │      URGENCY RATING (RING ONE)   1  Implement now and re-run │  │
│  │                                     system                │   │
│  │                                  2  Implement before next system use │
│  │                                  3  Implement as soon as possible │
│  │                                  4  Non-urgent request    │   │
│  │                                                           │   │
│  │      USER AUTHORIZATION. . . . . . . . . . DATE. . . . . . │   │
│  └──────────────────────────────────────────────────────────┘   │
└─────────────────────────────────────────────────────────────────┘
```

SYSTEM MAINTENANCE CONTROL

SERIAL NO. . . . .

A AMENDMENT REQUEST

DIVISION/DEPT . . . . USER/ACCOUNT CODE. . . . .

SYSTEM(S) REQUIRING AMENDMENT . . . .

DESCRIPTION OF AMENDMENT (USE ADDITIONAL SHEETS AS NEEDED)

URGENCY RATING (RING ONE)
1 Implement now and re-run system
2 Implement before next system use
3 Implement as soon as possible
4 Non-urgent request

USER AUTHORIZATION. . . . . DATE. . . . .

B DEVELOPMENT ESTIMATE   (outline amendment description and specification attatched)

	MANPOWER	EXPENSES	COMPUTER USAGE	TOTAL
ANALYSIS	. . . . . .	. . . . . .	. . . . . .	. . . . .
DESIGN + SPECIFICATION	. . . . . .	. . . . . .	. . . . . .	. . . . .
PROGRAMMING + TESTING	. . . . . .	. . . . . .	. . . . . .	. . . . .
INTEGRATION + VERIFICATION	. . . . . .	. . . . . .	. . . . . .	
TOTALS	. . . . . .	. . . . . .	. . . . . .	[ ]

ESTIMATE AUTHORIZATION . . . . DATE. . . . .

C ACCEPTANCE OF ESTIMATE

USER AUTHORIZATION . . . . DATE . . . .

D AMENDMENT COST STATEMENT

	MANPOWER	EXPENSES	COMPUTER USAGE	TOTAL
ANALYSIS	. . . . . .	. . . . . .	. . . . . .	. . . . .
DESIGN + SPECIFICATION	. . . . . .	. . . . . .	. . . . . .	. . . . .
PROGRAMMING + TESTING	. . . . . .	. . . . . .	. . . . . .	. . . . .
INTEGRATION + VERIFICATION	. . . . . .	. . . . . .	. . . . . .	[ ]

CHARGE AUTHORIZATION. . . . . DATE. . . . .

Figure 7.13   *A maintenance control document*

context and it is unlikely that the arrangements made for handling maintenance work will differ from those made for other forms of development.

Maintenance staffing

Maintenance activity (referred to in Chapter 3 as tactical development) presents a paradox. It is unglamorous but requires a thorough knowledge of the application area and of the hardware environment, together with a brisk but methodical approach to testing and implementation. The problem is therefore that some of the best system development staff must be deployed in maintenance. Additional difficulties may arise if tactical development staff report (as is perfectly reasonable) to the computer operations manager.

A carefully thought out staff structure can help to offset some of these difficulties. The secondment into maintenance work of staff from a team which has just successfully implemented a new application is one useful way of circulating people through this function. Another approach could be by adding attractions, for example by offering more integrated responsibility, or the possibility for sectional responsibility.

Audit and evaluation

To ensure the well-being of an organization and its various functions the generation of an atmosphere of critical observation is essential. Many ambitious claims are made for information systems (they are 'faster', 'cheaper', 'integrative'). It is therefore appropriate that these systems come under regular scrutiny. There are several forms this scrutiny can take.

Post-implementation evaluation looks at the impact which the new system has had for its users.
Regular internal audit is a continuing assessment of the role played by the system within the organization.
Regular external audit is a periodically obtained independent view of the part played by a system in satisfying the interests of the shareholders, public sponsors or other benefactors.
Function audits are reviews of the whole of computer development or computer services undertaken from time to time. An individual system may be viewed in this wider context.

These different forms of scrutiny have different objectives, are performed by different people and will employ different techniques. The features of the techniques and their overlaps is shown in Figure 7.14.

The techniques of audit

It is possible to approach the audit task in three different ways.

Procedure checks
Using *test data* to verify that the procedures and programs of the system operate correctly.

Data checks
Using special auditing packages to verify that the data stored in the system is as it should be.

System checks
Examining the system as a system with special emphasis on its own internal controls for consistency and checking.

A combination of all three techniques would provide the basis for an effective audit. In performing the audit, use will be made of any facilities which the thoughtful designer has incorporated into the system. The existence of audit trails and file reconciliations is an obvious example. In addition the availability of a totally comprehensive transaction set (including a 'mirror image' for each transaction) will greatly assist the audit process. Many other techniques exist including the provision of special marker fields in all data sets to allow traces to be performed. These are specialist matters for a systems design text and will not be considered further here but it is clear that 'auditability' is yet one more criterion to be used to define quality targets for a system design.

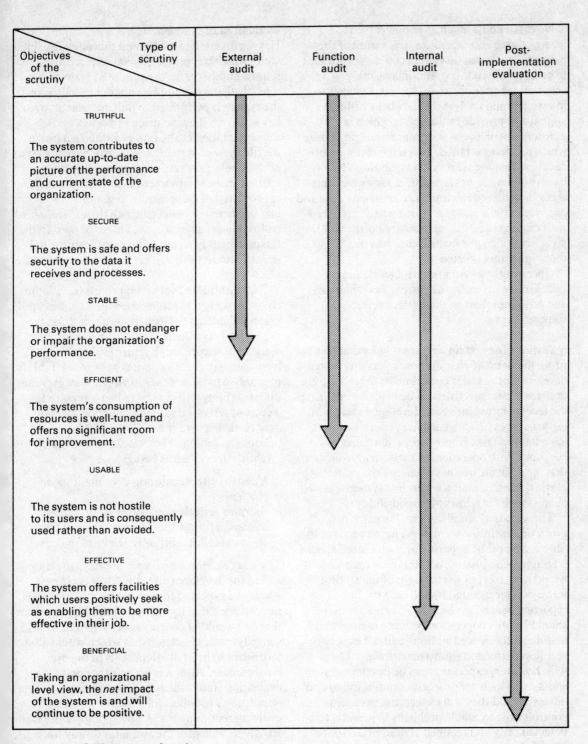

Objectives of the scrutiny / Type of scrutiny	External audit	Function audit	Internal audit	Post-implementation evaluation
TRUTHFUL The system contributes to an accurate up-to-date picture of the performance and current state of the organization.				
SECURE The system is safe and offers security to the data it receives and processes.				
STABLE The system does not endanger or impair the organization's performance.				
EFFICIENT The system's consumption of resources is well-tuned and offers no significant room for improvement.				
USABLE The system is not hostile to its users and is consequently used rather than avoided.				
EFFECTIVE The system offers facilities which users positively seek as enabling them to be more effective in their job.				
BENEFICIAL Taking an organizational level view, the *net* impact of the system is and will continue to be positive.				

Figure 7.14   *Different types of scrutiny*

No matter how much attention is paid to incorporating audit facilities, the nature of the process is such that no system could ever attempt to be fully self-auditing. It is increasingly common for auditors to use special packages to interrogate and analyse the data held within a system and provide for sampling which is independent of any of the programs or procedures which are being audited. Given the diversity of data base management systems, auditors may have problems in achieving this. However, once access is achieved, auditors can aggregate data and produce various analyses which when compared with calculated results or industry norms will yield lines of enquiry which can then be thoroughly investigated.

Operating at a system control level, auditors can examine critically the system's components and offer comment on their effectiveness and completeness.

Implications for system development management

From the point of view of those managing systems development, a major contribution to satisfying external audit objectives can be made by ensuring the incorporation into each developed system of those features, discussed above, which facilitate the auditor's task. Another contribution is to cooperate with operations management to ensure that the difficult area of system maintenance, particularly the interface with live systems, is well defined with clear lines of responsibility.

Those audits (usually internal ones) which probe deeper into systems – perhaps even into the functioning of the department itself – need special attention. The systems development manager would be correct to ask for sight of the auditor's terms of reference and understand the line of reporting which is to be used. Thereafter there should be full cooperation between manager and auditor. Experienced auditors will not expect seamless perfection from a department. They will, however, expect there to be development standards which are properly communicated and observed, and they will expect that management controls exist to enable problems in projects to be detected early and rectified at minimum risk to organizational investment.

Evaluation of systems

Having invested in a deep and thorough feasibility study which has produced a set of carefully refined objectives for the proposed system, it is sensible that, once implemented, an evaluation of the system is performed to find out exactly what it has achieved. The inclusion of post-implementation evaluation as a standard phase in the life cycle of systems will clearly have the effect of sharpening the realism of initial objective setting. In an environment where user managers are required to demonstrate to senior management the benefits which their system has realized, one can expect the language used in the feasibility study report to be more realistic and sensibly cautious than if no such review ever takes place.

Establishing an evaluation project has a lot in common with performing the initial studies for a project. The same objectivity is needed and the same openly conducted investigation required. This is not surprising, because evaluation is to look critically at a functioning system, and this is precisely what is done when an old system comes under scrutiny with a view to being replaced. Terms of reference for the evaluation must be very clear, because there is potential for misunderstanding. The evaluation could seek to establish the system as being:

Harmless safe, secure and does not impede efficiency
Accepted actively used by its users
Successful fulfills the original objectives set for it
Relevant fulfills currently relevant objectives.

The last criterion seems very unfair to the user and to the development team. How can a new system be expected to respond to circumstances not considered in its initial design? The answer is that one would of course expect a system to have some dynamic characteristics which would allow it to adapt to most developments in the user environment. Also, it is wasteful to conduct an evaluation study which does *not* use the opportunity to collect information about users' evolving requirements. A good compromise is strictly to segregate the evaluation study findings. A clear statement concerning the extent to which

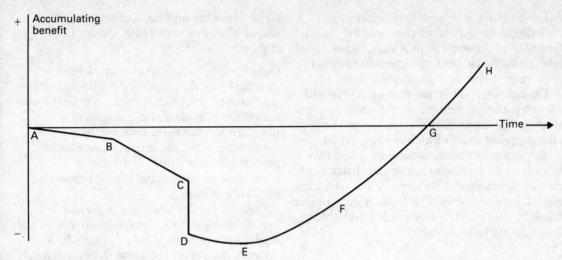

Figure 7.15   *Accumulating benefit of a project*

the system fulfills its original objectives should be made and, in addition, recommendations given for amendment and enhancement in the light of newly perceived requirements. Conducting the study has much in common with conducting a feasibility study (refer to Chapter 2).

The timing of the evaluation is critical. The accumulating benefit for a typical information system investment is shown in Figure 7.15. Money flows *out* during *AB* (manpower expenditure on analysis and design), *BC* (manpower expenditure on construction) and *CD* (expenditure on special hardware requirements). At *E* the system goes live and during *EH* the benefits of using the system offset its running costs, eventually recoup the initial investment (at the break-even point *G*), and go on to yield a steady positive cash flow illustrated as *GH*. Choosing the right time to mount the study depends on what we expect to measure. If it is required to establish that the system is *harmless* or *accepted* then the study could be mounted somewhere around *F*. If however, we are required to establish *successful* or *relevant* status it will be necessary to wait until after the *G* point. The financial judgements used should be the ones employed to assess the project's worth in the feasibility report.

Conducting an evaluation study has been compared to conducting a feasibility study.

However, one unique aspect of evaluation work must be stressed; giving feedback on the effectiveness of the estimating techniques used as part of the feasibility study. The following areas can be contrasted as shown in Table 7.4.

Table 7.4   Estimated and actual system features

Estimated manpower consumption during development	v	Manpower costs booked to the project
Lines of code estimated as being required in the developed system	v	Aggregated program source code sizes in the implemented system
Hardware configuration and costs estimated for the proposed system	v	Sizes and costs of hardware units needed to support live system
Estimated running costs (including staff reductions proposed)	v	Actual costs of operating and maintaining the live system
Proposed increased income due from, e.g. improved sales turnover	v	Changes to income attributable to the effect of the newly implemented system
Discussion of unquantified benefits expected, e.g. improved communication, better customer service	v	Statements from users concerning the impact of the new system on job efficiency and effectiveness

This feedback is invaluable in helping the evolution of the techniques employed for feasibility assessment and provides another justification for conducting a careful analysis of implemented functioning systems.

The end result of evaluation work is to provide a statement concerning the system which has been studied. The statement will often give guidance on appropriate actions which can be taken to correct any identified shortcomings. These may be sufficiently detailed to justify an enhancement project. Alternatively, the scope of the statements may identify a complex of difficulties and a proper feasibility study will then be needed to establish how they will be overcome.

Redevelopment of systems

An evaluation may identify that a major rethink is required within an application area. The circumstances that may precipitate this are numerous, for example:

Strategic The benefits accruing from use of the current system may be small and the original objectives may no longer be strongly desirable.
Efficiency Running costs may have escalated.
Technology Evolution in hardware or software within the organization demands that the base of the system is changed.

Edict Major organizational change (e.g. a takeover) may prompt a new, standardized approach.

Once the redevelopment of an application is indicated then the proper approach is to re-enter the standard development cycle, probably at the feasibility study stage. Redevelopment is therefore handled in the same way as development, and the same conditions must prevail, i.e. clear terms of reference, a representative study team, precise objectives, open style of working.

Care needs to be taken that important opportunities to revise the system are not missed. If, for instance a new standard approach to financial control is to be adopted, perhaps it may be a good idea to consider a fourth generation software tool for some of the development work. Conversely, if the refit is for technological reasons, it may be sensible to incorporate new or modified user requirements at the same time. In summary, the biggest danger to redevelopment of an applications area is that it might take place in a blinkered fashion ignoring the opportunity to advance on all fronts. The way to overcome this is to ensure that full development disciplines are applied so that both user and developer are able to influence the upgrade.

Exercises

1 Is it likely that attitudes towards systems (i.e. acceptance or resistance) would differ in the various environments defined below? If so why?
   a) New transaction input styles for bank clerks.
   b) New computer reporting for factory operators.
   c) New stocktaking methods for retail warehousemen.
   d) New financial reporting standards for divisional directors throughout the organization.
2 In Figure 7.6 a form of training is defined which results in know-how being transmitted down a hierarchy of staff. Identify some problems which this form of training could cause and describe safeguards which would prevent these problems.
3 User groups which are deeply dependent upon their existing systems will find it impossible to accept major changes to them using a parallel run approach because of time constraints. Describe how the dramatic Big Bang approach can be moderated.
4 Identify factors which could be used to decide that a system should no longer be adjusted by a maintenance request procedure but instead be considered for complete redevelopment.
5 A systems development department has a good

reputation for the quality of systems implemented but a very poor record of achieving either the costs or the timescale

originally planned. What auditing procedures would you adopt to help trace the root of the problem?

Further reading

Chambers, A., *Computer Auditing*, Pitman 1981

Mumford, E., *Values Technology and Work*, Martinus Nijhoff, 1981.

Hussain, D., Hussain, K. M., *Information Resource Management*, Irwin, 1984.

Outline solutions to exercises

Chapter 1

1 The organization can benefit by close attention to two areas. First it should ensure prompt payment to suppliers and sub-contractors. Secondly, it should ensure that all these costs are presented for government stage payment as soon as possible.

High priority applications: goods inward receipt and inspection, purchase control, contract costs posting, contract invoicing.
Lower priority applications: sales analysis, stock control.

2 *Information systems director*
Communication between IT units can only be achieved if they are all part of a strategy.
There is a negotiating benefit in going to suppliers with the fullest picture.
Common needs may identify where sharing of units may be possible.

Engineering director
Explaining technical needs to laymen is time-wasting.
CAD work is not data processing, and although interfacing to other systems is on the list of requirements it must *not* become an obstacle to buying the best CAD station that one can find.

Production director
It is not sensible to instruct managers on how they should spend small sums of money.
At very low levels of expenditure there are widely diverse requirements which individual managers understand and they should be allowed to satisfy them as required.

3 Strategy teams
Public lending library: Chief Librarian (chair), cataloguer, desk librarian, council official (libraries), council official (finance), DP consultant, finance officer, borrower (academic), borrower (leisure).

Technical college: Principal (chair), finance officer, DP consultant, student admin officer(s), lecturer (junior), head of a department, student (full-time), student (part-time), employer/sponsor.

4 a) Decentralization of the use of information systems can still occur with fully centralized computing facilities. It will be necessary to use accurate charging mechanisms, probably relying on usage details available from operating systems. Development staff could still be spread out into the operating divisions leaving only a skeleton central staff to support and maintain the centralized hardware.

b) It would seem that three potential environments exist for the system; defined microcomputers, as yet unknown microcomputers (in new acquisitions) and manual operation.

Thus the designers need to specify the system at a number of levels and must adopt formats and data storage definitions which are simple enough to suit the most unsophisticated file handling systems and which can be emulated at low volumes by clerical efforts.

There will be considerable pressure from users of the more capable microcomputers to elaborate the systems.

5 a) *See overleaf.*

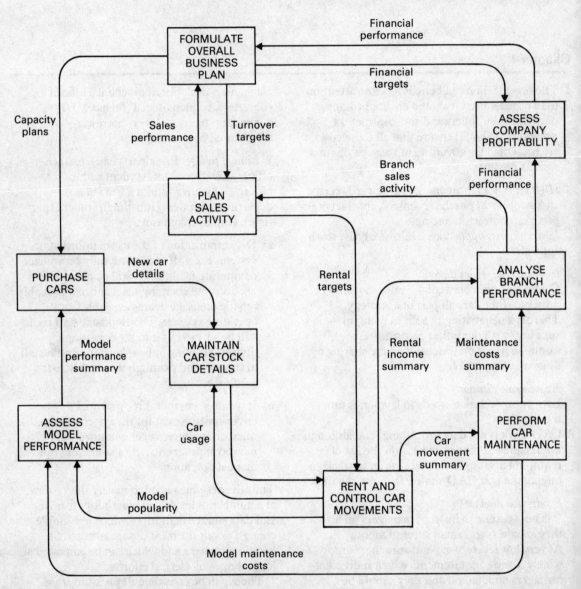

5.a *Information system set – car rental firm*

Chapter 2

1 Objectives:

a) That the transaction steps involved in dispensing should be simple and few, in order that users are encouraged into regular use of the system.

b) That the availability of the working dispensers at each site achieves the following pattern after one month of initial operation:

At least 75% of devices at a site available for 99% of each 24-hour, 7-day week.

At least 25% of devices at a site available for 99.75% of each 24-hour, 7-day week.

c) That the response time for each phase of interaction between the customer and the dispenser (card check, litre input acknowledgement etc.) is less than one second for 99.9% of interactive phases.

d) That high integrity over data recording should be achieved such that dispensing without data recording is impossible and that the loss of data through logical or physical failure is reduced to an extremely low level.

		This year	*Next year*	*Year 3*
CURRENT APPROACH	Manpower	30 000	33 000	36 300
	H/W Maintenance	3 600	4 500	9 500
	S/W Maintenance	2 000	4 500	10 000
	Total	35 600	42 000	55 800
	Cumulative	35 600	77 600	133 400
FIRST SOLUTION	Manpower	30 000	16 500	18 150
	Hardware		50 000	
	Software		20 000	
	H/W Maintenance	3 600	1 000	1 100
	S/W Maintenance	2 000	1 200	1 320
	Total	35 600	88 700	20 570
	Cumulative	35 600	124 300	144 870
SECOND SOLUTION	Manpower	15 000	16 500	18 150
	Hardware	60 000		
	Software	25 000		
	H/W Maintenance	1 500	1 650	1 815
	S/W Maintenance	1 200	1 320	1 452
	Total	102 700	19 470	21 417
	Cumulative	102 700	122 170	143 587

2 Neither purchase option breaks even at three years.

The immediate purchase option looks the better over the period concerned. The underlying trend of costs is better for the deferred purchase option due to the apparently lower maintenance charges.

3

		Year 1	Year 2	Year 3	Year 4
Costs	Hardware	100 000	—	—	—
	Hardware maintenance	10 000	11 000	12 500	14 000
	Software	25 000	—	—	—
	Software maintenance & enhancements	—	10 000	3 000	5 000
	Total costs	135 000	21 000	15 500	19 000
Benefits	Stock reduction	—	150 000	—	—
	Credit control	5 000	—	—	—
	Sales improvement	—	20 000	30 000	35 000
	Total benefits	5 000	170 000	30 000	35 000
	Cash flow	(130 000)	149 000	14 500	16 000
	Discount factor	1	0.909	0.826	0.751
	Discounted cash flow	(130 000)	135 441	11 977	12 016
	Net present value	29 434			

For the leasing arrangement

		Year 1	Year 2	Year 3	Year 4
Costs	Hardware	36 000	36 000	36 000	36 000
	Hardware maintenance	10 000	11 000	12 500	14 000
	Software	25 000	—	—	—
	Software maintenance & enhancement	—	10 000	3 000	5 000
	Total costs	71 000	57 000	51 500	55 000
Benefits	As above				
	Total benefits	5 000	170 000	30 000	35 000
	Cash flow	(66 000)	113 000	(21 500)	(20 000)
	Discount factor	1	0.909	0.826	0.751
	Discounted cash flow	(66 000)	102 717	(17 759)	(15 020)
	Net present value	3 938			

4 Risk areas for this user are:

1 No development staff in-house, therefore no experience of development issues.
2 Users not experienced with systems.
3 There will be integration of areas currently operating with some degree of independence.
4 All hardware and software components will be new and untried for this environment.

The risks should be offset by appropriate measures.

Start with education to promote awareness of the capabilities of information technology. Demonstrations, visits and videos should be useful.

Secondly, conduct a critical organizational review of current (manual) systems, with the objective of establishing what they do and where they fail. This should involve all principal users and lead to heightened organization awareness.

Then consider engaging consultancy assistance with the immediate objective of specifying requirements for the introduction of computer systems. A phased approach to hardware and software introduction will enable the equipment to be assessed prior to more extensive investment. Initial selection of a small project will also lessen the impact of failure due to user or equipment problems.

5 RFQ
Using an RFQ approach implies that detailed knowledge of the intended system is possessed by the purchasers. This could arise because:
1 The system is already in operation and is not to be changed.
2 The system is simple in scope and lends itself to ready estimation of technical requirements.
3 The system has some very critical

performance aspects (often timing), and the user has taken care to research these thoroughly and understands the technical specification needed to support this required performance.
4 A proposal has been received from one supplier with a full equipment specification and the purchaser wishes to obtain comparative quotations from plug-compatible manufacturers.

Chapter 3

1 *Arguments in favour of accepting outside work*
Produces income for the organization.
Operating in the real commercial world could improve the computer division's efficiency.
Helps to level out troughs and peaks in the internal workload.
Helps to retain the more ambitious and capable staff within the organization.

Arguments against accepting outside work
Internal requirements could begin to rank lower than lucrative external opportunities.
Staff expertise may develop in directions not relevant to internal needs.
A stronger commercial operation would have to be set up including a proper sales order/invoicing procedure.

The organization as a whole would be diversifying and would acquire responsibilities which it may regret.

2 a) Preliminary study of the product literature would highlight areas where interest or queries exist. The consultancy could be sent an example system from the organization and asked to prepare and present their product in this context.

The following interested personnel could form an audience for the demonstration: The systems development or strategic development manager, to balance the price/effectiveness of the product and assess its universality; some strategic development project leaders and analysts, to assess the ability of the product to adapt to a variety of design requirements; some tactical development section leaders and analysts, to assess the contribution to system documentation which the products would make, and the consequent impact on maintenance tasks; and the quality control officer, to explore the contribution which the product could make to achieving and monitoring the development of high quality systems.

b) Some initial contact would give guidance on the stage to which systems were developed in the new unit. Three people with good experience of user contact who also have the objective of building good early relationships with the new unit would be: one of the strategic development project leaders, who may have to begin an investigation into some systems problem already current in the unit; the user liaison officer, who will be responsible for user satisfaction at this new site; and the information centre manager, who will be promoting independent development work and providing support for it.

3 Devolving the budget can increase the coordination responsibilities of the manager because several people now need to be monitored. However, it has the potential of easing the management process because some decisions about quality and timescales will be taken at lower levels. The systems development manager will need to operate monthly budget review meetings. Candidates to be responsible for their own budget could be:

Strategic development manager: To be responsible for costs of staff and hardware deployed on major active development projects.

Personnel officer: To be responsible for staff training expenditure.

Tactical development manager: To be responsible for costs of staff and hardware deployed in the enhancement and maintenance of live systems.

Support manager: To be responsible for costs of staff, hardware and tools in general support work

Information centre manager: To be responsible for costs of staff and hardware used to support user-developed systems.

4 It will be necessary to regulate each cycle of the prototype process. Standards drawn up with reference to the technique should establish:

1 The tools preferred to produce the prototype required at each cycle.
2 The extent of the documentation (if any) needed to accompany each cycle of the prototype development.
3 The process needed to evaluate each prototype.
4 The documentation and operational characteristics which any prototype would require before it could be acceptable as a live running system.

To ease the burden of documentation, emphasis should be placed from the beginning of the development on embedded descriptions, diagrammatic techniques and the evolution of a data dictionary.

5 *Head of information services*
Provides staged standard outputs which simplifies management.
Aids future maintenance and therefore durability of systems.

Assists communication between analysts.

The analysts/designers
Encourages rigorous analysis of current systems.
Illuminates the important discussions between user and developer.
Provides standard specifications for programming.

User managers
Projects will be more structured and thus more manageable.
Implications of design suggestions are more easily explored.
Better system documentation is protection for their investment in systems.

Chapter 4

1 The main difference between the late phases of projects and the earlier ones is in the proof that they are in any way complete. The act of testing and installing computer systems requires that some measure of correctness is established. Early phases do not meet the same test and can often slip by because there is pressure to get on with construction. These early phases can be checked by the team leader, who looks at the quality and penetration of the specification, and the quality control officer who checks that all the required deliverables from a phase exist and are of acceptable standard.

2

Number of teams M	Size of teams N	Intra-team communication lines $I=\frac{1}{2}N(N-1)$	Total for all teams $T=M\times I$	Communication between team leaders $L=\frac{1}{2}M(M-1)$	Total for pool $=T+L$
1	24	276	276	—	276
2	12	66	132	1	133
3	8	28	84	3	87
4	6	15	60	6	66
6	4	6	36	15	51
8	3	3	24	28	52
12	2	1	12	66	78
24	1	—	—	276	276

A structure with six teams each of four members gives the minimum number of total lines of communication.

3 The benefits
   a) The ability to select the organization and the proposed team which offers the best service.
   b) The certainty of expenditure which can then be confidently planned.
   c) The accountability of the whole computer services operation.
   d) The ability to call upon particular expertise as and when required from within the consultancy service.

Circumstances which favour the approach:
   a) When an old system has to be maintained alongside a totally new one.
   b) When a restructuring of the organization requires that a centralized computer unit has to be reduced.

c) When a newly acquired part of the organization is to be rapidly standardized with the computer service operation.

4 Evaluate a new software product for screen formatting:

Read specification and clarify operation with suppliers, 2 days

Agree evaluation criteria with users, 2 days

Perform tests within the evaluation schedule and record results, 4 days

Prepare draft report, discuss with supplier and adjust according to any additional information, 4 days

Finalize report, include recommendations and circulate, 1 day

Total 15 days

Train stock recording clerks to use new system:

Assess ability/experience of clerks, familiarize self with typical user source data and prepare dummy input documents, 4 days

Inspect and finalize user guides, 1 day

Prepare and give overview presentation, 2½ days

Prepare and conduct working demonstrations, 3 days

Support casual training usage by clerks, 2 days

Total 12 days

5 Project completion time is now 70 (was 67). The critical path is now B-E-G-H-I-K.

Modified recedence network for Question 5.

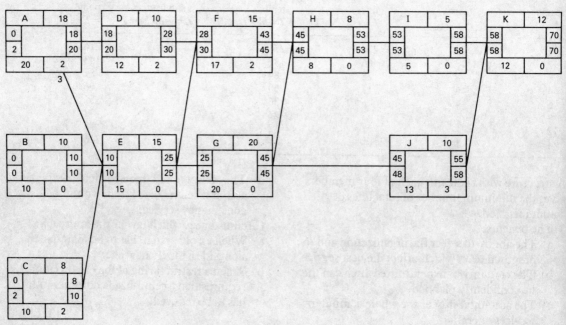

Chapter 5

1 When aggregated over a period of time the sheets provide a useful comparison between categories of work, including percentages spent on current designated projects, intruding projects (support or maintenance), and on non-productive activities (training, meetings). This data should be used to improve global estimating for future projects.

Task monitoring can be conducted by looking at tasks which are now complete, tasks scheduled to finish but not finished, and tasks scheduled to start but not started.

As a team leader who wished also to check on overrunning (or projected overrunning) tasks you would need to have ready access to orginal task estimates, time spent in prior periods and timesheets of others sharing the same task (if any).

2 *Progress review personnel* Senior executive (Chairman), project leader with other project members as appropriate, project secretary/ planner, quality control officer, systems development manager and/or information systems manager, computer services or operations representatives as required, and supplier representatives if appropriate.

Agenda
1 Minutes and matters arising from previous meeting.
2 Review of actions placed.
3 Project leader's statement, circulation of progress statements (cost summary, networks).
4 User representative's statement on progress, discussion of project objectives.
5 Quality control officer's statement on achievement of project to date.
6 Supplier's or operations statement as needed.
7 Any other business.

3 a) Where there is a rigid, external deadline, for example decimalization day, the Stock Exchange Big Bang.
b) Where accuracy and robustness are paramount, for example in space missions, medical equipment, bank cheque clearing systems.
c) Demonstration systems which are urgently required but will not survive for long need not be highly maintainable or secure.

4

Schedule efficiency (S)	Cost efficiency (C)	Forecast efficiency (F)	Revised forecasted efficiency (R)
70	90	99	70
75	80	91	61
81	72	83	60
98	63	75	59
106	65	78	60
126	68	64	62
140	.70	65	65
154	70	65	65

4 *cont.*

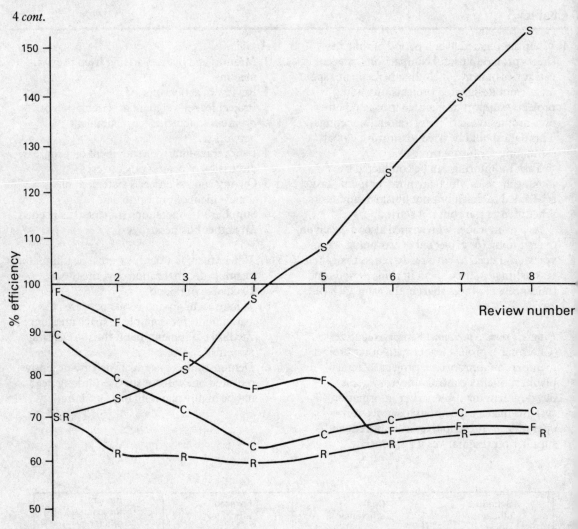

Efficiency indicators for Question 4.

The project starts badly with insufficient committed resource (S). The indicator (R) immediately suggests poor performance, and over the next three reviews there are worsening cost and forecast indicators (C and F). Once additional resource is committed and trained (by review 5) the indicators, and the project, settle down until completion.

You should recommend that, in the early stages either the project should be replanned to tackle the resource problem or the allocated resource should be protected from interference. Also the induction of the new programmer should not be charged to the project cost but be allocated under a training budget.

5 *Technical*:
  U User interaction experience
  N Some analysis and design experience
  N Some programming and construction experience
  U Some managerial or leadership experience
  U Knowledge of capabilities and limitations of current equipment

Personal:
N Actively seeks and performs well in
  interpersonal communications
N Has well-developed critical faculties
N Is respected by colleagues

U Diplomacy
U Is a good listener

Key U = useful
      N = necessary

Chapter 6

1 Employment in a team helps to satisfy:
  Social interaction The individual can interact
  with others to obtain benefits from discussion
  and is made to feel part of the bigger successes
  that are obtained by combined efforts.
  Social recognition Good performance in a team
  leads to recognition, giving a feeling of worth to
  the individual.
  Self-fulfillment Team membership provides
  opportunities for the practice of leadership,
  advice and liaison, mediation and other social
  skills.
      Team membership subordinates the
  individual to group goals and group cooperative
  effort. The best practitioners may resent the
  requirement to slow down in order to achieve
  common progress, and the need to spend time
  communicating may be resented by those in a
  hurry to crack the next technical puzzle.

2 The large demand for systems development
  staff and the consequent shortage promotes
  mobility of labour. Staff may therefore seek
  career development by changing employers
  rather than by promotion within a single
  organization. To facilitate this movement they
  may concentrate on transferable technical
  accomplishments rather than get involved in
  fundamental organizational objectives. This
  will be seen as a lack of enthusiasm for the
  interaction and debate required to tackle broad
  issues. The buoyant market for computer staff
  can lead to the situation where staff seek to
  influence their current job development to suit
  the demands of the external market. Their
  selection of training courses and the degree of
  enthusiasm they display for assigned tasks are
  influenced by these ulterior motives and may

not, therefore, align with the organization's
objectives. Those managing the systems
development function should be aware of this
difficulty. If unconventional products are used
for development work, staff may feel isolated
from the larger information systems
community. On the other hand, if development
work is on mainstream products then staff
marketability will be high and turnover can be
expected to occur.

3 a) The participator style is appropriate. There
     are the twin objectives of speed and
     acceptance to be reconciled. The manager
     can achieve this by having an active role, and
     by involving the programming team leaders
     in the evaluation and selection process. Too
     much delegation might result in inadequate
     momentum being generated. Too little
     involvement by team leaders may result in
     their rejecting the 'imposed' solution.
  b) The salesman style should be useful. A new
     team of effective people has to be selected
     for the information centre. The manager
     must ensure that these are the best for the
     job and that their own career development
     plans are in harmony with this move. There
     is the worry that the project leaders may
     suffer conflicts of interest if involved too
     closely in the establishment of the new
     team.
  c) Delegator would probably work in this
     context. The manager is happy, in principle,
     with the proposal. After defining terms of
     reference for his team leaders he could ask
     them to work with the quality officer to
     achieve the definitions required.

4 a) The inexperience of the appraiser.

   The difficulty of having a frank discussion of personal weaknesses in a situation where the senior programmer may feel that the project leader is not sufficiently experienced.

   The problem of generating ideas that will stimulate what has perhaps become a career without much direction.

  b) The appraisee's lack of understanding of the appraisal process and what may be gained from it.

   The lack of a substantial record of progress or achievement for the appraisee. Few details of personal as opposed to technical weaknesses are available.

  c) There may be little new to say about the appraisee's personal weaknesses, and any actions which could improve them.

   The frustration of the appraisee with his career stagnation may create an awkward discussion, which is not conducive to positive thinking.

   The difficulty of agreeing a development plan which does not lead in an obvious way to opportunities for extended responsibility.

5 The most capable designer or programmer has little value if he cannot find a way to contribute as part of a team. Personality clashes not only waste time but can interfere with people's objectivity, disrupting ordinary communication at work. Good team work produces output which is greater than the sum of the members' individual potential, whereas a fraught team will have depressed output. Recruitment of a poor team worker is not only a waste of an appointment but can upset a currently productive group.

A candidate's suitability for team effort can be assessed at various stages in the selection process. The application form may show high job turnover; the interview by technical management, with its detailed discussion of the cv will give clues about the candidate's social skills; the group session with potential teammates will provide an opportunity to assess the candidate's approachability and response to gentle social enquiries; and finally the panel interview will provide the opportunity to explore particular points of interest in the candidate's history which have been highlighted during the earlier sessions.

If there is too much concentration on social acceptability then a manager runs the risk of failing to appoint sufficient people of high ability or dynamism. Instead he may build groups of people who are pleasant but may lack the flair which could raise their overall potential.

Chapter 7

1 a) A major part of the bank clerk's job is the capture of data and the accurate recording of it. It is to be expected that a positive atmosphere will prevail assuming job losses are not involved.

  b) Shopfloor operators are employed to manufacture; data recording is of minor importance. Their attitudes may be either neutral, or potentially negative if extra work is involved, or if suspicions about management use of the data are aroused.

  c) Like bank clerks, warehousemen see data recording as a major component of their job. There will be an approach of positive criticism to the efficiency of the new method.

  d) Directors will fully support new systems which are intended to increase effectiveness – but they will be critical, and may be obstructive, if heavy demands on their time are required or sharp deadlines imposed.

2 *Accuracy* At each step the information being passed down could become distorted in some way resulting in an inaccurate set of instructions being passed on at the last stage.

Indifference Information that is of special interest to clerks may be passed to them by supervisors whose interests in the system may lie elsewhere.

Time The technique is serial in the sense that several layers of people have to absorb information in turn before the process is complete. This could take a long time.

Safeguards are accurate user guides, booklets, slides, OHP transparencies and wall charts, which give details of the operation of the system. If it is necessary to check the accuracy with which all the users have been prepared, systems development staff can monitor the inputs made during pilot or parallel phases and correct any misconceptions which are apparent from this study.

3 The deeply committed user may have to go for a Big Bang, but everything should be done to ensure that the new system will operate with a minimum of problems. As well as the organization of acceptance and training sessions it should be possible to: arrange pilot sites, where new techniques are tested in real situations; schedule dummy runs where the complete work force can be immersed in the new system without abandoning the old; seed support staff into user departments during the early live usage stage; and provide 'hotline' support for serious difficulties. One could also have a contingency plan for the reinstatement of the old system.

4 The following factors could be weighted and scored for an application to judge its suitability for redevelopment:

1 The continuing importance of the application area to the organization's business objectives.
2 The continuing importance of the application area to the user department.
3 The degree of fit between the system characteristics and the current development methods.
4 The cost of annual maintenance work normally performed on the system.
5 The expected cost of maintenance work forecast for future periods.

5 The reputation for quality should be investigated to see whether clues emerge by that line of investigation. Generally the areas to audit are:

1 The standards used for project life cycles (i.e. estimating; planning; monitoring, reviewing).
2 The influence of users within the project life cycle – are they controlled or do they overwhelm?
3 The quality control function – are its findings traded against project progress or accepted unquestioningly?
4 The amount of management training or education invested in systems development leaders.
5 The efficiency of the service provided for systems development by operations.
6 The morale and motivation of systems development staff.

Index